D1287059

IT HAPPENED ON THE UNDERGROUND RAILROAD

Tricia Martineau Wagner

TWODOT®

GUILFORD, CONNECTICUT
HELENA, MONTANA
AN IMPRINT OF THE GLOBE PEQUOT PRESS

A · **T W O D O T**® · **B O O K**

Copyright © 2007 by Morris Book Publishing, LLC

TwoDot is a registered trademark of Morris Book Publishing, LLC.

Front cover photo: *The Underground Railroad*/Chas. T. Webber. Library of Congress,
LC-USZ62-28860
Text design by Nancy Freeborn
Map by M. A. Dubé © Morris Book Publishing, LLC

Library of Congress Cataloging-in-Publication Data
Wagner, Tricia Martineau.
  It happened on the Underground Railroad/Tricia Martineau Wagner.—1st ed.
    p. cm.
  Includes bibliographical references and index.
  ISBN-13: 978-0-7627-4001-7 (alk. paper)
  ISBN-10: 0-7627-4001-9 (alk. paper)
  1. Underground railroad—Anecdotes. 2. Fugitive slaves—United States—
Anecdotes. I. Title.
  E450.W14 2007
  973.7'115—dc22
                                                        2006020770

Manufactured in the United States of America
First Edition/First Printing

To my husband, Mark Wagner,
whom I'd marry all over again.

I consider involuntary slavery a never-failing fountain
of the grossest immorality, and one of the deepest sources of
human misery; it hangs like the mantle of night over
our republic, and shrouds its rising glories.

—Reverend John Rankin, 1826

CONTENTS

CONTENTS

ACKNOWLEDGMENTS

I gratefully acknowledge the assistance of the following people, without whom I could not have written this book:

- Diane Miller, National Program Manager, National Underground Network to Freedom, Omaha, Nebraska, for her research assistance and direction on the Underground Railroad.
- Caroline R. Miller of the Bracken County Historical Society, Brooksville, Kentucky, for her invaluable research on Arnold Gragston, Reverend John Rankin, and John P. Parker, and also for compiling census records from the Freedom Center in Covington, Kentucky.
- Anne-Marie Rachman, Michigan State University Library, Special Collections, for her research expertise, especially the information she uncovered about James Lindsey Smith.
- Marla Baxter, Assistant Director of Tourism & Renaissance on Main, Lynn David of the Museum Center, and Betty Coutant of the *Mason County Beat* in Maysville, all of whom shared their information on Arnold Gragston.
- Betty Campbell, president of the Board of Trustees for Ripley Heritage, Inc., and member of the Board of Trustees for the John P. Parker Historical Society, Inc., for sharing research on Reverend John Rankin. Her presentation on John P. Parker inspired me to write about him.

- Major Ronald J. Rice of the Maysville Police Department, for sharing research material on Arnold Gragston and for inviting me to visit the Broadway Christian Church in Dover, Kentucky.

- Doris E. Onorato at the Van Allen House Heritage Center in Mount Pleasant, Iowa, for collecting a plethora of information on Ruel Daggs.

- Mary Savage, the museum board historian for the Lewelling House and Quaker Museum; and Faye Heartsill, president of the board at the Lewelling Quaker Museum, Iowa, for sharing material on Ruel Daggs.

- John Zeller, research historian for the Antislavery and Underground Railroad Project of the State Historical Society of Iowa, for general information on the workings of the Underground Railroad in Iowa.

- Joan Beaubian, president of the New Bedford Historical Society and cofounder of the Massachusetts Underground Railroad Network, for providing information on Nathan and Polly Johnson.

- Jennifer Bergeron of the Barney Ford House Museum in Breckenridge, Colorado, for research on Barney Ford.

- Erin H. Turner, my editor at the Globe Pequot Press, as well as Allen Jones, whose expertise fine-tuned this manuscript into a book.

- The staffs at the Hege Library at Guilford College in Greensboro, North Carolina; the University Library at the University of North Carolina-Chapel Hill; and the Rare Book Manuscripts and Special Collections Library, Duke University, Durham, North Carolina, for their research assistance.

- Peter Jareo, library supervisor of the Carmel branch of the Public Library of Charlotte & Mecklenburg County, North Carolina, for his research assistance. Also to his staff for ordering countless interlibrary loan books from libraries around the country.

ACKNOWLEDGMENTS

- Natalie Mikysa, Senior Reference Assistant of the Main Library of the Public Library of Charlotte & Mecklenburg County, North Carolina, for her research assistance.

- Gaye E. Gindy, Sylvania historian, Sylvania, Ohio, for her willingness to share her wealth of information on the Lathrop and Harroun families. Her research did much to prevent the Lathrop House from being razed.

- Polly Cooper, Sylvania Area Historical Society, Sylvania, Ohio, and Catherine Martineau, Esq., for information on the Lathrop House.

- My friends Amy Norman and Sherry Williams, who assisted with ordering books needed for my research.

- Sharon Sacksteder, FSIL, for sharing the story of Miss Edith May Haviland, her remarkable fifth-grade teacher at Lincoln Elementary School in Adrian, Michigan. The work of Miss Haviland's abolitionist ancestor, Laura Smith Haviland, was thus brought to my attention.

- Beth R. Olsen, author and long-distance friend, who suggested that I write this book, for her encouragement and her research assistance on William and Ellen Craft, and for helping to unravel the quilt myth and its connection to the Underground Railroad. I also thank her daughters, Andrea Cramer and Julia Smoot, for the same.

- Melissa Johnson, for her continuous support and for accompanying me on visits to Underground Railroad sites. Everyone should be blessed with a friend like her in life.

- My husband, Mark, for his technical support and unending patience, and our children, Kelsey and Mitch. Thank you for being such a loving family.

- For graciously granting the author their time for interviews: Baloyan, Greg; Baxter, Marla (Assistant Director of Tourism and Community Development, Maysville, Kentucky); Coutant, Betty (the *Mason County Beat,* Maysville, Kentucky); David, Lynn (Museum Center, Maysville, Kentucky); Edwards, Lee; Gindy, Gaye E. (historian, Sylvania, Ohio); Johnson, Reverend William; Miller, Caroline (Bracken County Historical Society, Kentucky); Rice, Major Ronald (Maysville Police Officer); Schmidt, Eva; Still, Clarence Harrison Jr.; Williams, Brenda Rice.

INTRODUCTION

Far from being truly underground, or even a railroad, the Underground Railroad was in fact a loosely organized network of individuals who assisted slaves as they escaped bondage in pre-Civil War America. Between the 1820s and 1860s, an untold number of enslaved African Americans fled from the South to seek their freedom, mostly in the northern United States or Canada. As rail transportation became increasingly popular in the 1830s, metaphors emerged to describe the movement. "Passengers" escaped along "lines," transported by "conductors" and aided by "agents" who had made the arrangements. The "stations" were safe houses where the fugitives hid and were offered food, clothing, and temporary shelter.

There are several claims as to the origin of the term "Underground Railroad." One involves a slave named Tice Davids, who ran away from Kentucky to Ripley, Ohio, in 1831. When Davids's owner could find no trace of him, he said that his slave had "gone off on an underground road." By the 1840s most people knew the name, Underground Railroad, and were aware of the existence of a hidden network of individuals, families, and small groups taking in slaves who came to them from the previous station and making sure that they made it to the next.

It was never a large-scale operation with membership or national regulation. Most "conductors" knew only a handful of people involved with the railroad, and very few were familiar with an entire route. Given the constant threat of fines, imprisonment, or even death, it was work that had to be done in the utmost secrecy.

The period of greatest activity for the Underground Railroad began with the passage of the Fugitive Slave Law of 1850. With this new law slave owners could legally pursue their runaways even into the free states of the Union, capturing them on free soil to take them forcibly back to a slave state. Ironically, the passage of this law only strengthened the abolitionist movement and bolstered the determination of those activists involved in the Underground Railroad.

Even aided by the Underground Railroad, slaves on the run often had to rely on their own resources. To outwit the bounty hunters and their bloodhounds, they sometimes camouflaged their scent by running through a river or a creek, or rubbed their feet with onion, pine sap, or pepper. Often they were not dressed appropriately or suffered from hunger and other privations. Very few had money, and most were unable to read road signs. Uncertain of whom they could trust, they were in constant fear of being caught. If they were captured, punishment was swift, often in the form of severe, potentially fatal whippings. For some slaves, however, the fear of being sold to the Deep South, with its reputation for cruel treatment, was a threat worse than whipping.

The Underground Railroad encompassed multiple routes to freedom over land and water. Most slaves who escaped north to Canada or the free states came from the border states, their proximity to free soil increasing their chances of success. Slaves from Texas, however, often crossed the Rio Grande into Mexico. Some groups of fugitives set up self-sufficient "maroon societies" in remote areas such as the Great Dismal Swamp along the Virginia and North Carolina border. Slaves from Georgia, South Carolina, and Alabama sometimes escaped to live with the Seminole Indians in Florida or the Caribbean, while others sought out black communities where they could blend in with those already free.

Historically there has been an overemphasis on the participation of white abolitionists in the Underground Railroad, and an underrepresentation of involvement by African Americans. Typically traveling at night, fugitives might get a head start if they left on a Sunday or a holiday, when their absence might not immediately be noticed. Young men statistically had the highest chance of success. Unencumbered by family, they could cover greater distances. They were also more often familiar with the surrounding area, especially if they had been hired out on various jobs around the community. Once they connected with a "conductor," however, typically they put their lives in the hands of a complete stranger. They would be taken along various routes, sometimes zigzagging or backtracking to throw off any slave catchers on their trail. Most conductors could take them only as far as the next station (anywhere from ten to thirty miles). On each stage of the journey, they might hide in wagons with false bottoms or inside caskets, or they might walk beside a casket as if participating in a funeral procession. If their light skin allowed them to "pass" for white, they might look for a nice set of clothes and try to board a train or boat to freedom. Some fugitives even had themselves mailed north.

While accurate statistics are unavailable (to protect the participants, most of the paperwork was either nonexistent or destroyed), it is estimated that less than 2 percent of America's four million enslaved people ever escaped to their freedom. The "father of the Underground Railroad," William Still, in the course of his work for the Philadelphia Antislavery Society, did manage to preserve an accurate record. Much of what we know today about the Railroad today is due to his diligence.

Harriet Tubman, Frederick Douglass, Levi Coffin, and Sojourner Truth are a few of the famous names associated with the Underground

Railroad, but there are a host of unsung heroes as well, all with inspirational stories. Individuals such as John P. Parker, Seth Concklin, Peter Still, and the Rankin family often risked their own freedom and health by assisting others in their escapes from bondage.

The institution of slavery, from its start in 1619 to the end of the Civil War in 1865, is an unspeakable stain on America's history. The true stories contained in *It Happened on the Underground Railroad* are tributes to the courage of those—enslaved and free, black and white, women and men—who devoted their lives to helping others obtain their freedom.

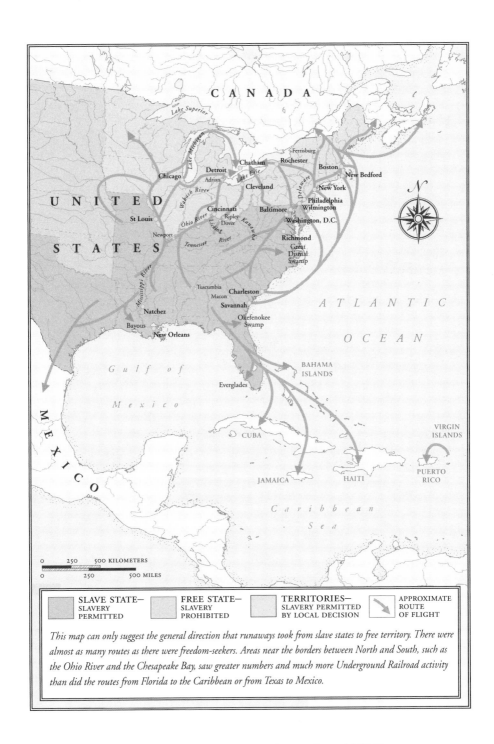

CANADA

Lake Superior

Lake Michigan

Chicago

Detroit Chatham Rochester Boston

Adrian Lake Erie New Bedford

UNITED Cleveland New York

Wisbish River Philadelphia

Cincinnati Baltimore Wilmington

St Louis Ripley Washington, D.C.

Ohio River Dover

STATES Newport Licking Richmond

Tennessee River Kanawha Great
Dismal
Swamp

Mississippi River

Tuscumbia Charleston

Macon

Natchez Savannah

Bayous Okefenokee
Swamp

New Orleans ATLANTIC

OCEAN

Gulf of BAHAMA
ISLANDS

Everglades

Mexico

MEXICO CUBA VIRGIN
ISLANDS

JAMAICA HAITI PUERTO
RICO

Caribbean

Sea

| | SLAVE STATE— SLAVERY PERMITTED | | FREE STATE— SLAVERY PROHIBITED | | TERRITORIES— SLAVERY PERMITTED BY LOCAL DECISION | APPROXIMATE ROUTE OF FLIGHT |

This map can only suggest the general direction that runaways took from slave states to free territory. There were almost as many routes as there were freedom-seekers. Areas near the borders between North and South, such as the Ohio River and the Chesapeake Bay, saw greater numbers and much more Underground Railroad activity than did the routes from Florida to the Caribbean or from Texas to Mexico.

0   250   500 KILOMETERS

0   250   500 MILES

SELECTED ROUTES OF THE
UNDERGROUND RAILROAD

ON A DARE

It was well after midnight when John Parker crept up to the back of a slave owner's house in Kentucky and slipped through the kitchen door. As his eyes adjusted to the gloom, he saw the light of a candle shining out from underneath a bedroom door. He imagined he could hear snoring. It seemed like a simple enough mission. All he needed to do was sneak undetected into that bedroom, steal an infant, and then find a way to make his exit without being detected and shot. Mindful of the squeak of floorboards, he took another careful, heavy step into the room.

John P. Parker had grown up an angry child. At eight years old, having just been separated from his mother and forced to walk from Norfolk, Virginia, to Richmond in a chain gang of slaves, his anger was directed at anything that, unlike him, was free. After Richmond he was sold to a slave trader and suffered the indignity of being shackled to others once again and marched another eight hundred miles to Alabama.

As he grew older, John Parker became a determined, hardworking, intelligent young man. He eventually mastered the skills involved with iron molding and was often hired out to work elsewhere. He saved every penny that came his way until, by age eighteen, he was able to purchase his freedom. In 1848 he married and settled in Ripley, Ohio, a bustling river port fifty miles east of

Cincinnati. Standing on the north bank of the Ohio River, he could look out over the slave state of Kentucky.

John Parker came to own his home as well as an iron foundry in Ripley, where he employed both black and white workers. He was seen as a well-regarded, upstanding citizen. During the day he ran his business. At night, however, he became a slave runner. Nearly every evening while his family slept, he would walk out his front door and pursue his clandestine work as an agent and conductor on the Underground Railroad.

When confronted, Parker adamantly denied aiding fugitive slaves. During one of his many forays into Kentucky, however, he noticed a poster with a thousand-dollar reward for his capture, dead or alive. Apparently people had their suspicions. Parker refused to be intimidated. Instead he armed himself and learned the habit of walking down the middle of the street, day or night, so that he could not be abducted into an alley.

In the mid-1860s a white employee at Parker's foundry, Jim Shroufe, baited him, challenging that if Parker was so brazen, he should prove it by stealing some of Shroufe's father's slaves in Kentucky. Parker outwardly ignored the man, but secretly took the dare.

That very night John Parker rowed quietly across the Ohio River, tying off his boat and stealthily making his way up the steep, tree-lined bank below Shroufe's house. This first attempt, however, wasn't meant to be. In the darkness, following a form down a dirt road, he soon saw that he was mistakenly following a white man. He feared that it might be one of Shroufe's other sons, John, who was a slaver patroller east of Dover, Kentucky, and not someone Parker wanted to run into. Parker narrowly escaped this unwanted encounter and, for the moment, aborted the rescue mission.

Three nights later, Parker was able to identify himself to one of Shroufe's slaves and reveal his plans. The man had a small family, and explained that he could not leave without his wife and baby. Parker agreed to take them all the following week. Just as they were finalizing the plans, however, a slave patroller appeared out of nowhere and attacked Parker with a club. Parker threw dirt in his assailant's eyes and made a run for the river, rowing home while the slave took off for his cabin. The following day Jim Shroufe did not seem to have any knowledge of the incident.

The next week John Parker again rowed across the river, silently dipping his oars, propelling himself closer to possibly losing his own freedom. After the boat was hidden from the prying eyes of the patrollers, he went to find the young family.

Parker soon learned that Mr. Shroufe had been growing suspicious. To prevent the slave family from running away, Shroufe and his wife were keeping the couple's baby in their own bedroom at night. A gun and a candle were on a chair next to their bed.

Since the slave mother and father would not leave without their baby, the only solution was for Parker to sneak into the Shroufes' bedroom and snatch the baby right out from under their noses. The slave mother, who worked in the main house, described the layout of the two-story brick home. Parker instructed the parents to be ready to flee as soon as he returned with their baby. So that he could move quietly in the house, he removed his shoes and gave them to the man for safekeeping.

As Parker entered through the kitchen door at the back of the house, he let his eyes adjust to the sliver of candlelight coming from the bedroom. He eased barefoot across the rough plank floorboards. Carefully, he tried the latch on the bedroom door. On his third attempt the door creaked slowly open. It sounded very loud, but the heavy breathing inside assured him that the Shroufes were still fast asleep. After surveying the room, Parker noticed that Mr. Shroufe was lying nearest the door. The candle on the chair illuminated not one but two pistols.

Parker surmised that the baby was on the woman's side of the bed. As he lowered himself to the floor and crawled forward, the bedroom door swung shut behind him. Undaunted, he reached up for the bundle on the bed, pulling what he hoped was the baby toward him. The bed creaked loudly. Parker felt sure he had been discovered. He grabbed the baby and bolted for the door.

A chair crashed to the floor behind him, extinguishing the candle. The startled Mr. Shroufe felt around in the darkness for his weapons. Parker raced out the door, clutching the child. Together with the baby's parents, he ran toward the river. There were pistol shots, and bullets whined over their heads. As they ran past the slave quarters, the parents yelled that they needed to go back to their cabin for something. Parker kept running, calling back that if they wanted to see the baby again, they had better follow him. The couple ran after him down to the Ohio River—a distance of about a thousand feet. There was another boat at the landing, and they pushed it adrift so that it could not be used in a chase. Tumbling into Parker's skiff, rowing across the Ohio River in the dark, Jim Shroufe's voice could be heard from the dock, angrily calling the name of his father's escaped slave.

John Parker rowed upriver instead of directly across to his house. When they landed, Parker asked for his shoes. Unbelievably, the man claimed to have dropped them along the way. An infuriated Parker knew that his shoes could identify him. If convicted of assisting with a slave escape, he could have all his possessions confiscated and receive a prison sentence of up to twenty years. However, he had time only to concentrate on the task at hand, which was to make this newly rescued family disappear.

Parker took the fugitives to an abolitionist lawyer friend who would forward them on. With that done, Parker then ran to his house, undressed, jumped into bed, and waited.

Before he'd hardly had time to catch his breath, there was a pounding at his front door and angry voices demanding to see him. Parker came to the bedroom window in his nightshirt, seemingly irritated to have been awoken. Jim Shroufe was surprised to see Parker at home. Still he accused him of stealing his father's slaves, including the baby. Parker acted like Shroufe was out of his mind and purposely took his time getting dressed. Parker did not usually allow slave hunters to search his home, but now he wanted to give the fugitives a head start. After an exhaustive search Jim Shroufe and his father, pistols in hand, were sorely disappointed not to find their slaves.

The next day a triumphant Jim Shroufe showed up at work carrying Parker's shoes. Parker claimed never to have seen them before. Shroufe went to every shoe merchant in town, hoping to snare Parker, but no one gave Parker up. The defeated, disgruntled employee never came back to Parker's iron foundry again. He knew as well as Parker did that the man, woman, and baby were well into their two-hundred-fifty-mile journey to Canada.

John P. Parker and his wife, Miranda, had eight children, all of whom were eventually college educated. He owned a foundry, a blacksmith shop, and a machine shop, and was one of few black men before 1900 to receive patents for his inventions (including a portable screw tobacco press and a clod-smashing machine). For nearly fifteen years he had courageously put his life on the line in the name of freedom, successfully bringing at least one thousand men, women, and children to freedom's shore. It was his way of dealing with his "eternal hatred of the institution" of slavery. The angry little boy had grown into a man who devoted his life to liberating the oppressed and preventing the strong from destroying the weak.

WHAT GOES AROUND COMES AROUND

JUST AS MATTIE JANE JACKSON WAS WALKING UP the plank to the ferry that would lead her to freedom, she felt the cord around her waist loosen. The bundle of clothes hidden beneath her hoop skirt had begun to slide slowly to the ground. Mattie tripped slightly over the tangle at her ankles, but tried to act as if nothing was wrong.

Mattie J. Jackson was born into slavery in 1846 in St. Louis, Missouri. She had tried to escape numerous times over the years but had always failed. On previous attempts, however, she and her family had relied on no one but themselves, and she had gradually realized that to be successful, she would probably need assistance from others. Her current master and mistress, Captain and Mrs. Ephraim Frisbee, were much improved over an earlier master, Captain Tirrell, and far better than Mr. and Mrs. Lewis, who had beat her unmercifully. But by age seventeen Mattie was determined to have her freedom at last.

Mattie knew her best opportunity would be during one of those occasions twice a month when she was allowed away for two hours to go to church. These excursions became fact-finding missions, and soon enough Mattie had learned of some black folks who helped fugitive slaves. A plan was concocted, and Mattie was told that she had to adhere strictly to the schedule. Things had to run like clockwork if they were to succeed.

The escape plan was six months in the making. When the day finally came, however, everything seemed to go wrong. It was a Sunday, and Mattie had asked permission to attend church service. But it seemed that Mistress Frisbee was suspicious of Mattie's eagerness and would not allow her to go until all of her work was completely done. Master Frisbee then joined in with his own requests, purposely delaying her departure.

At long last Mattie retired to her quarters and set the plan into action. She tied nine articles of clothing, which was all she owned, into tidy bundles and attached them to a thin cord tied around her waist. Mattie had to make sure that the dangling packages did not distort the evenness of the circular hoops of her skirt. As it would be impossible to replace her meager wardrobe, Mattie was left with no choice but to take the clothes with her. She practiced walking around the small room thus attired.

Just as Mattie was finally ready to leave, she was called upon to dress the Frisbees' young son for a family carriage ride. As she attended to the boy under the watchful eyes of Mistress Frisbee, Mattie backed into a corner, putting the boy between her and the woman. When exiting the room, Mattie was very aware of the clothes dangling under her dress, and of the thin cord biting at her waist.

Later, as Mattie was walking on the road, the Frisbee family's carriage sped past her in a cloud of dust. Mattie picked up her pace.

Coming into town, Mattie saw a man on the opposite side of the street who appeared to be waiting for no one in particular. As she drew near, the gentleman turned and walked ahead. As planned, Mattie followed him at a safe distance. As they approached the church, the man dropped off to the side. Mattie stayed and waited for her next connection. Twilight began to spread over the small Missouri town. She soon noticed two young ladies chatting quietly. When Mattie walked up to them, one discreetly slipped a pass into

Mattie's hand and told her to follow along behind, leaving a considerable distance between them.

They led her to the river where a ferry awaited. Trying to look as if she rode on boats every day of her life, Mattie fell in line behind a group of Union soldiers. She presented her pass with an air of confidence, though she could not hear a thing above the beating of her heart. The ticket agent simply nodded her on. The plan seemed to be progressing without a hitch.

It was then that Mattie felt the rope around her waist begin to loosen.

Feeling the clothes slip from position, Mattie tried not to panic. The last thing she wanted was to draw attention to herself. Some soldiers nearby noticed her slight stumble but then turned away again, lost in conversation. With the bundle of clothes now at her feet, Mattie stooped slightly, maneuvering her hoop skirt in such a way as to allow her to push the bundle along with her feet, first one foot then the other, in slow, steady movements. Finally she found a seat out of the way, calmly sitting down as if nothing out of the ordinary had happened. When no one else was nearby, she would have a chance to rearrange herself.

As Mattie floated away on her ferry, and later as she boarded the rail cars that would take her to freedom in Indianapolis, Indiana, it was probably hard for her to believe that her dreams were finally coming true. Seven previous escape attempts with her mother had all failed. Over the years they had been sold, kidnapped, and resold. They had endured hateful masters and vindictive mistresses, and now it was all almost over.

Mattie J. Jackson went on to find much happiness in her life. Her sister, mother, and brother would also eventually make it to freedom. In Lawrence, Massachusetts, she would be reunited with her stepfather and his wife, who would help Mattie publish her life story.

In a strange twist of fate, some years later Mattie and her mother came across their former master and mistress, the cruel Lewises, on the streets of St. Louis. Mrs. Lewis had been so severe that she had often beaten them both at the slightest provocation. Mattie's mother recognized Mrs. Lewis at the market; Mrs. Lewis and her children were in a much-reduced station, being now forced to "wait upon themselves." Mr. Lewis was quite astonished to see Mattie, and inadvertently dropped her a bow before realizing who she was. The only thing Mattie then had to conceal was a smile.

IN THE DARK OF NIGHT

FIFTEEN-YEAR-OLD ARNOLD GRAGSTON SLOWLY PUSHED the skiff away from shore, being careful not to let the bottom scrape on the beach. Even in the dark of night, Arnold and the girl he was with hunkered low in the boat. He silently pulled the oars through the water, working against the current. Arnold's arms trembled from the strain. He would have loved to have looked into the gorgeous brown eyes of his sweet passenger, but he settled instead for feeling her eyes upon him.

A life lived in slavery or in freedom could be decided by as little as which side of the river you were born on. A slave in Kentucky only needed to cross the Ohio River to reach Ohio's free soil. Arnold Gragston had never considered doing it himself, but then he was asked to do it for someone else. Just the thought of it terrified him.

Arnold Gragston lived on Walton Pike in Mason County, Kentucky. Born on Christmas Day in the early 1840s, he was one of ten slaves belonging to Colonel John "Jack" Tabb, whose farm was between Germantown and Minerva. Arnold found Master Tabb to be a "pretty good man," as he gave relatively few beatings. He permitted his slaves to be taught to read, write, and figure, even though fellow farm owners looked down on it. He also did what he could to see that husbands and wives either worked on the same farm or, at the very least, lived together at the end of the day.

Arnold was a quick learner and was often hired out by Colonel

Tabb to other farms. Consequently, he had freedom to travel during the day. He was also allowed quite a bit of liberty at night, which meant that he could "go a-courtin.'" Little did Arnold know that his courting on one particular night would lead him to become part of a network that helped liberate slaves.

One evening in 1859 Arnold headed out to a nearby farm to call upon a pretty girl. Arnold was slight of build and not very tall, but he had spruced himself up to make a good impression. The old woman who answered the door, however, had plans other than accepting suitors. She explained to Arnold that she wanted him to row the girl across the river to Ohio.

Arnold was taken aback by the request, and his mind churned with the dangers inherent in such a mission. Too frightened to speak, he began to take his leave, but then the girl came to the door. She was "such a pretty little thing—brown-skinned and kinda rosy." The young Arnold Gragston was fixated and couldn't help but listen as the old woman laid out the details of the escape. The young girl's eyes betrayed how frightened she was.

No matter how smitten, Arnold just could not bring himself to take such a risk without first mulling it over. As hard as it was to believe, the grandmother said that there were white folks in Ohio who actually helped slaves escape. Arnold had no peace of mind that night as he envisioned himself undergoing the lash at the hands of an enraged master or, worse yet, being shot and killed for his part in a foiled escape.

Tabb's farm, where Arnold lived, was six miles directly south of Dover, Kentucky, a tobacco port on the Ohio River. Dover would be their point of departure. About a mile and a half east, across the river in Ripley, Ohio, the Reverend John Rankin, a Presbyterian minister, and his wife, Jean, would receive the girl and help move her on to the next station.

The Rankins' house sat far above the Ohio River, visible in an open clearing of trees and with a lantern shining brightly in a window every night. All Arnold had to do was row the girl across the river, look for the house with the light, and listen for a bell tinkling in the air. He was assured that the Rankins had people on the bank of the river waiting to direct fugitive slaves up the hill to safety.

The next evening Arnold Gragston found himself back at the old woman's house, the big-eyed, beautiful girl staring at him. The two teenagers made their way down the steep bank of the river, climbing into a waiting skiff and pushing away from the shore. Arnold glanced nervously around. Even a direct line across the Ohio River seemed a great distance. As he rowed in the stiff current, the night so dark that their progress was hard to determine, and the minutes felt like hours. At last Arnold saw a light high on the hill, beckoning to them like a lighthouse.

Arnold slid the skiff silently ashore. At that moment two men appeared and grabbed the girl, pulling her from the boat. Arnold trembled with fear and began to pray. Someone grabbed his own arm and said, "You hungry, boy?" The last thing he had expected was being offered something to eat.

The girl was in good hands now. Arnold turned around and rowed himself back to Kentucky, hoping that he would make it home undetected. The pretty girl was gone forever. She was well on her way to freedom, and Arnold was headed home with plenty to think about.

Although it took a while for Arnold to recover from his terrifying first trip across the river, he eventually realized that he could do it again. It came to be a well-kept secret that he was willing to assist runaways across the river. Typically, he preferred to meet his passengers on the darkest nights when their features would be obscured and he would thus later have a hard time identifying them. As the forms came up to him, Arnold would whisper, "What you say?" and if the correct password was given—"menare"—he would take them across the river. Arnold never knew the word's meaning, but thought it might have been a biblical term, though no such word is known.

Arnold Gragston began making three to four trips a month across the Ohio River, rowing under moonless night skies. Sometimes he carried just a few people; other times his boat was full. Instead of gaining his own freedom, he helped others attain theirs. Over a four-year period, he helped liberate close to three hundred slaves, and never did he ask for anything in return.

In 1863 after rowing twelve fugitives across the river, Arnold was nearly apprehended. To avoid being caught, he hid out for weeks, sleeping in fields and in the woods. He was married by this time, and when an opportunity finally presented itself, he took his wife Sallie as his last passenger across the Ohio River. It seemed like he was pulling the weight of the world in the boat that night, rowing them toward the familiar light on the bank.

Arnold and Sallie Gragston went on to Detroit, Michigan, coming back to Bracken County, Kentucky, in the 1880s. They would have ten children and thirty-one grandchildren. Over the years Arnold would visit his family on land that had once been the Tabb farm. He would sit on the front porch, in a chair surrounded by his great-great-grandchildren, and retell the story of his first adventure across the Ohio River. Upon his death in 1938, well into his nineties, Arnold was fondly remembered as a wonderful storyteller.

The Broadway Christian Church in Germantown, Kentucky, where Arnold Gragston was both a deacon and cofounder, still holds monthly services to this day. A historic marker in Germantown, Kentucky, reminds everyone that Arnold Gragston's story was one of courage and hope. This well-respected, brave man was laid to rest in the Greenlawn Cemetery in Ripley, Ohio, where he had first rowed so many to freedom.

DOWNRIVER

JOHN FAIRFIELD WAS A MAN POSSESSED. He angrily pulled on his boots, grabbed his whip, and stormed out of his cabin. News that one of his two slaves had escaped was bad enough, but hearing that his boat was also missing infuriated him. He stomped down to the salt-works along West Virginia's Kanawha River, demanding that his remaining slave be summoned. In front of a gathering crowd, Fairfield accused the frightened man of being involved in the disappearance. He cracked his whip near the slave's head, ignoring the man's repeated denials of wrongdoing.

What the crowd around them didn't realize, however, was that Fairfield, the self-important businessman, was not really from Louisville, Kentucky, as he claimed. Nor was he using his real name. And the "slave" whom he was currently berating was actually a free man from Ohio.

John Fairfield was born into a slave-owning family from Virginia, but came eventually to disagree with his family's position on slavery. As an adult he helped a childhood friend, Bill, escape from his uncle's farm. From that point on Fairfield realized that liberating slaves was possible if one possessed a sense of adventure, a willingness to take risks, and a cunning mind.

By the 1850s, word of John Fairfield's daring exploits in assisting fugitive slaves had spread up North, and the demand for his services grew accordingly. His specialty was in reuniting families separated by slavery. When some freed slaves in Ohio continually solicited Fairfield to rescue their relatives left behind in Virginia, John finally agreed to help, although he knew he would need a foolproof plan to move such a large number of people.

The enslaved relatives he was seeking to free lived in what is now Charleston, West Virginia (at the time, it was still the state of Virginia), nestled in the lush Appalachian Mountains. They toiled at the saltworks along the Kanawha River, near present-day Malden. Posing as a businessman, John Fairfield took his two best "slaves" and went to investigate the Kanawha salt brines. He was told that the water along the Kanawha River was saturated with salt. Since the early 1800s more than 1,250 pounds of salt had been extracted every day. The wealthy businessman allowed himself to be convinced that it could be a lucrative investment. The plan would be for him to haul the salt downriver and sell it for a sizeable profit.

Fairfield came to know the local slaveholders well enough to gain their confidence. Soon Fairfield's men began to construct two boats that would be used to transport his salt. He oversaw the construction and commiserated with fellow slaveholders on the difficulties of managing their slaves. Meanwhile his two "slaves" were seeking out the relatives of the Ohio contingent and informing them of the escape plan.

On a designated Saturday night after the first boat was completed, one of Fairfield's "slaves" and another slave, both of whom had knowledge of boating, crept down to the dock. The river was dark under a moonless sky. They slowly untied the rope and listened intently for any sounds. When the coast seemed clear, the men pushed off and headed downriver, letting the swift spring current carry them along. After some distance they steered the boat to the bank and threw a rope to the men who appeared in the brush.

Quickly the boat was filled to capacity, with not a sound being uttered by any of the men or women who hunkered down to hide their heads from view. The boat drifted along, beginning its sixty-mile journey to the Ohio River and freedom.

The next day was Sunday. The owners of the missing slaves initiated a frantic search, but it proved fruitless. On Monday Fairfield's boat was also discovered missing. The slaveholders assumed that their slaves had stolen the boat in order to escape. They took off on their horses in hot pursuit. At the mouth of the Ohio River, they found Fairfield's boat beached on the opposite side. Of course there were no slaves to be seen.

John Fairfield made quite a scene about his boat being stolen. He was livid that his slave had most likely run off with the others. As his second boat neared completion, he vowed to watch his remaining slave like a hawk. Since he was quite the actor, no one suspected that Fairfield was involved in any way.

The following Saturday night Fairfield's second slave repeated the plan, absconding with an additional ten or twelve slaves. How they managed to slip away under Fairfield's watchful eye remained a mystery to the real slaveholders in Charleston.

When Fairfield was told that his second boat and slave were missing, his fury knew no bounds. He ranted and raved and complained that he was now ruined, and he joined the other men who set off to capture the slaves. They rode sixty miles, only to be disappointed. There on the other side of the Ohio River was Fairfield's second boat.

The men ferried across the Ohio and followed Fairfield's suggestion to split up in order to widen their search. By then, of course, the fugitive slaves had been forwarded along the circuitous path of Ohio's well-established Underground Railroad. When the pursuers met at the designated rendezvous point to confer on their findings, Fairfield was not present. He had disappeared. It was probably some time before the slaveholders realized they had been outwitted.

Sometimes it would take John Fairfield six months to assume a new role, establish himself in a community, and gain people's confidence. He masterminded countless schemes, posing as a slave trader, a slaveholder, or a businessman. Once he donned the attire of an undertaker and led twenty-eight slaves to freedom in a staged funeral procession.

Fellow abolitionists did not always condone Fairfield's methods of arming his fugitives and using violence if necessary, but they did admire his determination. Over a twelve-year period, he reunited families with their loved ones from almost every slave state. In all he helped to free several thousand slaves, forwarding most of them to Canada via the Underground Railroad.

Although his final fate is uncertain, it is likely that Fairfield died tragically during a slave insurrection in Tennessee. He fit the description of an unknown white male, new to an area on the Cumberland River, who was killed in a failed escape attempt of a large number of slaves. After 1861 he was never heard from again.

The peace-loving abolitionist Quaker Levi Coffin shared these words about John Fairfield: "With all his faults and misguided impulses, and wicked ways, he was a brave man; he never betrayed a trust that was reposed in him, and he was a true friend to the oppressed and suffering slave."

MY BETTER HALF

AFTER ALMOST ONE ENTIRE YEAR OF FREEDOM up North, "George" walked one hundred miles south, back into slave territory. As soon as he crossed the border he took up his former name Tom and sneaked into his wife's slave quarters after dark. He put his hand over her mouth so that she would not scream as she awoke, quickly outlined his plan to her, and then vanished back into the night.

One year earlier, in the autumn of 1846, Tom and a friend had escaped north, briefly hiding in the basement of Zion Baptist Church in Cincinnati, Ohio. The fugitives took new names and, after being fed and clothed by a white woman named Laura Smith Haviland, were secreted to another safe house. Mrs. Haviland, also known as "Aunt Laura," made arrangements for them to be taken on to a Quaker community eighty miles further north. She never expected to see either of them again.

Tom's friend continued on to Canada, but Tom remained among the Quakers, finding work and saving his wages. No one knew of his plans to return to slavery.

Nearly twelve months later he stole away in the dark of night, returning to Kentucky. His wife's plantation was eight miles away from his old master's property and he stopped there first. When he sneaked into her cabin that night, she almost fainted from the surprise of seeing him. Covering her mouth, he whispered in her ear, "I tell you, Liz, I ain't got whole freedom without you." He planned to ask his master to take him back, explaining to him that he was sick of freedom. Tom hurriedly explained his idea, then disappeared as quickly as he had come.

The next morning Tom walked up to the master's house, wearing the tattered clothes he had run away in. Master Carpenter was shocked to see him but even more stunned when Tom spoke. With a big grin Tom told his former master that he was happy to be back and that he never wanted to leave again. He claimed that the free black man was overworked and underpaid in the North. Tom shook his head and said, "Abolitioners the greates' rascals I ever seen. I wants no more ov' em. They tried hard to git me to Canada; but I got all I wants of Canada. An' I tell you, Massa Carpenter, all I wants is one good stiddy home." Then Tom fished the crumpled eighty dollars he'd earned out of his pocket, and with an outstretched arm, he said, "I don't want this money; it's yourn."

Master Carpenter was shocked but pleased that his former slave Tom had come back. He bragged of Tom's return to the neighboring planters, explaining that apparently Tom had left on account of a big fight with his wife. Even so the other masters found it hard to trust a runaway who had sampled a taste of freedom. Tom was warned that if he stepped onto his wife's plantation he would be shot. This gave Master Carpenter a good laugh, and he said, "You couldn't hire Tom to go near Liz."

Tom became as dedicated and trustworthy a slave as there ever was. At first Lizzie's master had bloodhounds trained to keep Tom off his property. Eventually though, her master became convinced of Liz's disgust with Tom, and he let his guard down.

After three months Master Carpenter's friends had heard enough good things about Tom that they had no objections when Carpenter allowed him to attend slave gatherings on neighboring plantations, letting him join in with the socializing, singing, and praying. Tom insisted on only attending day meetings so the owners could keep an eye on him. He was overheard telling other slaves how awful it was up North.

One day Liz raised a fuss about Tom's possessions he'd left in her cabin when he ran away. She made it known that she meant to burn them or pitch them to the pigs if he did not claim them soon. Word was sent to Tom to come to the meeting the following week for his things.

Tom's master instructed him to retrieve his clothes, perhaps so that he would not have to spend money replacing them. Tom dutifully obeyed and made his way to Lizzie's plantation. Seeing Liz, he caused a huge scene by hurling insults at her. She retorted with name-calling and said that his leaving did nothing to make her feel bad and she didn't care if she ever saw him again. Tom's feelings were clear: "I never wanted to see her face agin, an' we almos' cum to blows."

Tom and Liz saw each other infrequently and communicated only through a trusted messenger. Several months later the second phase of the plan was ready.

A holiday was approaching and Tom, who wished to visit his aunt, had no problem getting a pass from Master Carpenter. Likewise, Lizzie received a pass from her master to go see friends. Both left their respective plantations at dusk, with Tom heading six miles away in one direction and Liz walking five miles the other way.

They walked until it was dark. Then they each turned toward the Licking River in Kentucky, one of them walking upriver and the other downriver until they met. Away from the watchful eyes of plantation owners, they were free to embrace and speak lovingly to each other before quickly carrying out the third phase of the plan.

Tom searched the riverbank for a usable skiff. This took some time, since boats were often secured to the shore without oars, rendering them useless to possible runaways. After finding a skiff with oars, they jumped in, and Tom rowed off in darkness, pulling north for the Ohio River.

At daybreak they hid the skiff in the brush near the river's edge. They found cover farther inland, taking the oars with them. They felt safe until some mischievous boys stumbled across their skiff, using poles to propel it off the bank. It was a close call for Tom and Liz, who had almost been ferreted out while the boys searched for the missing oars.

After nightfall Tom and Liz searched again for a suitable skiff. Near midnight they found one. Once again Tom rowed hard until close to daybreak, when they approached the junction of the Ohio River.

Just when they thought their slavery was a thing of the past, two men beside the Licking River spotted them. They yelled out, asking where Tom and Liz were headed. Tom replied that they were going to market. After asking Tom and Liz what they were selling, the men began making their way to a boat at the water's edge. At that moment Tom knew he was in for the race of his life.

Forgoing polite conversation, Tom turned his skiff for Ohio's shoreline and took off, heaving at the oars with every ounce of strength he had. Even with freedom in sight, both Tom and Liz knew that if they were caught it would likely lead to a fate worse than death.

Tom gasped for breath, the sweat dripping off his flushed face and his muscles burning as if they were on fire. Halfway across the Ohio River, he nervously glanced behind him to see how close his pursuers were. Apparently, when the men had seen that they would not be able to catch Tom and Liz, they had turned back. Luckily they were not armed. Tom felt physically and emotionally drained but was thankful that he and Liz were out of immediate danger.

Once ashore, Tom led Liz to the Zion Baptist Church that had sheltered him the year before. They hid in the basement until Laura Smith Haviland came to see to their needs. "George" remembered Aunt Laura immediately and was quite excited to see her. Mrs. Haviland, in meeting so many fugitives, could not place him at first. Tom replied that he was none other than the man George who had come through last summer. He reminded her that she had given him the linen pants, blue-checked gingham coat, and straw hat that she had pulled from her large market basket. Mrs. Haviland remembered having arranged for the two men to be taken in a wagon to a Quaker community. When she asked how he came to pass through again, Tom replied, "It was for this little woman I went back."

Tom and Liz, renamed George and Mary, joined other fugitives that Laura Smith Haviland was conducting along the Underground Railroad through Toledo and then to Detroit and finally on to the safe haven of Canada.

There is no account of how Tom's and Lizzie's masters took the news of their escape. Master Carpenter was surely dumbfounded, if not embarrassed. And it must have brought a smile to Tom's face knowing that, through his fine acting, he had outwitted the lot of them. Apparently he had wanted something to do with Canada after all.

REMEMBER ME

WHEN THE DOOR TO WILLIAM STILL'S OFFICE ON North Fifth Street opened on August 1, 1850, it revealed a tall, middle-aged man named Peter Friedman. He had traveled hundreds of miles from Alabama to find his family and had been directed by local churches to the office of the Anti-Slavery Society. He was hoping they might be able to help him. But even in his wildest imaginings he couldn't have been prepared for what he learned that day.

Twenty-nine-year-old William Still wasn't yet known as the "Father of the Underground Railroad," but during his lifetime the energetic young black man would work his way up from being clerk, field organizer, and secretary, to chairman of the Acting Committee of the Pennsylvania Anti-Slavery Society. Currently, as secretary, his job was to personally interview fugitives who had made their way to Philadelphia, determine what assistance they needed, and keep a record of all expenditures. He would later record life stories so that family members could locate one another.

William listened attentively and took notes as Peter, nearly twenty years his senior, unfolded the saga of his life. As a free black man, it was hard for William Still to imagine undergoing such trials and tribulations as being sold like a piece of property and being beaten unmercifully. He seemed to have little in common with the man on the other side of his desk—or so he thought.

Peter, now fifty years old, had been separated from his mother for more than forty years. His early memories were admittedly dim when trying to recall exactly where they had lived or what his mother and sisters had looked like. The two men studied each other with regret. With so little to go on, it was doubtful there would be a happy ending to Peter's search.

Peter shared the main events in his life. He had lived the better part of it in Kentucky and Alabama, a slave under various masters. He was the second eldest of four children, and while his father had been able to buy his own freedom, Peter, his mother, and his siblings had remained slaves. He remembered one failed escape attempt when he was six years old, and vaguely recalled a kidnapping after which he and his brother never saw their mother and sisters again. Peter had suffered a terrible loss when his brother had died at the hands of a cruel master at age thirty-three.

It wasn't until Peter was an adult that he had been able to buy his freedom. Now he was seeking assistance for purchasing his wife and children, whom he had left behind in Alabama. Regrettably, Peter did not know his real last name; Friedman was the name of his last owner. He also could not say exactly where he had been born.

William Still mentally noted how his own life contrasted so sharply with that of the man sitting across from him. For one thing, William had been born in New Jersey and was raised free. He was the youngest of eighteen children. His deceased father, Levin, had purchased his own freedom when he was a young adult, but his mother Charity had been a runaway. She had escaped slavery with their two daughters, William's oldest sisters. Two sons, William's brothers, had been left behind in slavery. Charity had been reunited with William's father and had changed her name for safety's sake.

William Still needed more information, and asked Peter to recall any details that might provide some clues. Peter remembered that he had been five years old when his father had gone north. A year later, his mother had taken all four of her children with her on her first escape attempt. Peter was then six years old; his brother Levin was eight; and their sisters were younger. Their arduous journey to freedom was short-lived. It was somewhere along the Delaware River, perhaps near Philadelphia, that slave catchers had come in the middle of the night and abducted them all, dragging them back to their owner.

Peter's mother was locked up for three months to ensure that she would not run away again, but that did not deter her. A few weeks after her release, Levin and Peter had awoken to find her and their sisters gone. Out of spite, their enraged owner, Saunders Griffin, sold the confused and distraught boys to Kentucky so that their mother would never find them. Before they were taken away, the boys' grandmother told them never to forget the names of their parents, Levin and Sidney, and to remember that they were up north of the Delaware River.

William Still put down his pen and furrowed his brow as he listened further. Peter told about how he and his brother had been sold and resold, working in brickyards, tobacco factories, and cotton fields, sometimes enduring whippings at the hands of overseers and masters. As Peter talked about searching for his wife Vina and his children—Levin, Peter, and Catharine—a terrible sadness came over him. William had seen that same look on the face of his own mother, who often prayed for the two sons she had left behind.

It seemed that William Still did have some things in common with Peter Friedman after all. Peter kept mentioning the name Levin, which had been the name of William's father as well. Peter's mother's name was Sidney, which had been the name of William's mother before she had changed her name to Charity. Peter had been told to head for the Delaware River near Philadelphia if he was ever freed; William's mother lived near the Delaware River, on the east side in New Jersey.

William thought of his own mother as he stared at Peter. The brow line was nearly identical and the eyes had a familiar shape. The bridge of the nose was also the same, except that Peter's nose was somewhat broader. The lips were dissimilar, but both had high cheekbones, a trait inherited from ancestral intermarriage with the Lenape Indians.

William Still sat lost in thought. All he'd been told growing up was that his two older "lost brothers" had been sold to an unknown location. His mother had never stopped praying for . . . Levin and Peter.

William must have been dumbfounded when he heard Peter say the names of his two younger sisters. They were Mahalah and Kitturah, the very names of William's older sisters who had escaped with their mother.

William Still had been born twenty years after Peter. Nevertheless, how had he not seen the striking resemblance to his, to *their*, mother when Peter had first walked into his office? It was so obvious now. William later recalled, "My feelings were unutterable. I could see in the face of my newfound brother, the likeness of my mother."

Very slowly William said, "Suppose I should tell you that I am your brother?" Peter sat there speechless. Having known nothing but hardship and heartache all his life, Peter was amazed that he could have encountered such a stroke of good fortune. The very man helping him to find his family turned out to be a brother he never even knew existed.

Peter "Still," as he was informed his last name was (their father Levin had changed his last name from "Steel" to "Still"), had never been forgotten by his family. Their parents had gone on to have thirteen more children, although not all of them had lived to adulthood. Their father had died eight years earlier, but their mother was still alive. Their sisters, Mahalah and Kitturah, lived in Philadelphia. Three more of Peter's siblings lived nearby: Mary ran a school for black children in the city, and James (a doctor) and Samuel (a farmer) both lived in New Jersey.

Surely his newfound family must have seemed a miracle to Peter Still, who spent the next day meeting his five brothers and three sisters, all of them eager to see the older brother they had heard so much of. And we can only imagine Peter's reunion with his mother. Her aged hands trembling as she reached up to hold his still-familiar face. Peter felt his mother's frail embrace, and neither of them could contain their sobs.

The missing pieces of Peter's life came together. Peter had lived in Maryland as a child. On that first escape attempt, his family had made it to New Jersey before being dragged back. His mother had then made the heartrending decision to escape with his sisters and had kept it a secret for safety's sake. Unable to take all her children with her, she had kissed her sons good-bye as they had slept and put them in God's hands. Peter's grandmother had been right in saying to look for his mother near the Delaware River. His family was nearby in Burlington, New Jersey.

With the discovery of his mother and siblings, Peter's broken heart was half-filled with joy. The other half ached for his wife and children, who remained in bondage.

Only a week after the reunion, Peter Still returned to the McKiernon plantation in Tuscumbia, Alabama, where his family lived, carrying one hundred dollars that he had raised. His mission now was to try and bring his own wife and children north to meet the rest of his family.

MISSION IMPOSSIBLE

IT WAS A SUNDAY IN MID-MARCH, AND the boatload of fugitives had just noticed another skiff floating toward them down the Mississippi River. Concklin immediately quit the oars and loudly ordered "his slaves" to row harder. Vina and Catharine hid under blankets hoping that they had not been found out. A few hours later, fierce winds were nearly pushing their skiff toward the riverbank's lashing trees. What should have been a thirty-six hour trip to the Ohio River had taken fifty-two hours. The Stills could only hope that the close calls and delays thus far were not an omen of things to come.

In 1850 Seth Concklin had read a story in the *Pennsylvania Freeman* that incited him to action. A man named Peter Still had apparently been reunited with his mother and siblings after forty years of bondage, but Peter's wife and children remained slaves in Alabama. Even though he had never met the man, forty-eight-year-old Concklin decided to do what he could to liberate Peter Still's loved ones.

Seth Concklin had always felt sympathy for the oppressed. He had supported his widowed mother and siblings since the age of fifteen, often aided destitute strangers, and once rescued a man about to be lynched. It seemed a natural step for this unassuming and sympathetic man to join the growing ranks of the abolition movement.

Concklin contacted the office of Philadelphia's Anti-Slavery Society with an offer to rescue Peter Still's family in Alabama. He was told by William Still and J. M. McKim, who never consulted the rest of the Vigilance Committee, that agents were not sent south on rescue missions. The purpose of the office was to assist runaways who came to their town.

Meanwhile, after a failed trip to Tuscumbia, Alabama, to try to free his family, Peter Still had returned to Philadelphia. He was informed that a stranger named Seth Concklin had been offering to help his family escape. At first Peter was reluctant to accept Concklin's gracious offer, but seeing no other viable option, he finally agreed.

They decided that once in Alabama, Seth Concklin would assume the name of "John H. Miller," a slave owner traveling north with his slaves. Peter Still explained the layout of the plantation where his family lived and described his wife and children. He also gave Concklin the cape of his wife, Vina, in order to identify him to her as someone to trust. He also passed along the one hundred dollars he had earlier raised for his family's release.

In January of 1851 Seth Concklin began exploring possible river routes north from Alabama. He would take the Tennessee River to the Ohio, and then up the Wabash River into Indiana and on to Detroit, where they would cross into Canada.

On a rainy Tuesday in late January, Concklin arrived at McKiernon's plantation under the pretense of looking for work. With the aid of a slave, he set up a rendezvous with Peter's family. He identified himself to Vina and presented his escape plan to her and her three children—twenty-one-year-old Levin, nineteen-year-old Peter, and thirteen-year-old Catharine. (Eight other of their children had died.) They were to leave in four weeks.

Steamboats along the Tennessee River were unreliable, so Concklin went to Cincinnati to procure a skiff for their escape. On the same steamboat that he took to Cincinnati was Vina's master, Bernard McKiernon, totally unaware of the unfolding plot.

In early March when McKiernon was in New Orleans, Vina and her children met up with "John H. Miller" at 3:00 A.M. along the Tennessee River. They slipped into the waiting skiff, with Peter and Levin taking up the oars beside Concklin. By daybreak they were passing Eastport, Mississippi, where the river turned and headed north through Tennessee. It was just the beginning of a daunting and dangerous six-hundred-mile journey.

At one point during this first leg of the trip they narrowly missed passing McKiernon's steamboat as he returned from his trip. It was traveling up the Mississippi River from New Orleans and back down the Tennessee River to Alabama. Luckily Concklin and the Stills were on the other side of an island in the river.

It was soon afterwards that they had the close encounter with an approaching boat on the Mississippi. Concklin quit the oars as Vina and her daughter took cover. On Monday, March 17, they fought the fierce winds and avoided the rocky shore. At sunrise on Tuesday they set up the Ohio River, sixteen hours behind Concklin's time schedule. It was a seventy-five-mile row to the mouth of the Wabash and then another forty-four miles to New Harmony, Indiana, where they landed at 10:00 A.M. on Sunday, March 23. They had been rowing for seven straight days and nights.

Concklin's first concern was to throw off any slave catchers who might be on their trail. Once they left the river, Concklin found clothes more typical of free blacks rather than the rags common to slaves, and the weary band of fugitives began traveling on public roads to Princeton and Vincennes, Indiana. Over a five-day period, they stayed with various agents of the Underground Railroad prearranged by Concklin.

On Friday, March 28, while walking along the road, nineteen-year-old Peter helped retrieve a spotted runaway horse for its owner. Not long afterwards a man in front of a sawmill tried to start up a conversation by inquiring which way they were traveling. At night-fall the group stopped at another house in Vincennes, Indiana. Con-cklin went ahead to arrange the next stopping place, having no idea that leaving the Stills would be a costly mistake.

While sitting around a fire, Vina Still and her children heard the sound of horses' hooves outside. Seven men came to the door. One was the owner of the spotted horse; another was the man they had seen by the sawmill. Vina answered their questions, saying that they had come from Kentucky and were going to Springfield, Illinois. Their master had died, and they'd been left to his brother, John H. Miller. The rowdy white men were suspicious, perhaps because of the way the Stills were dressed. Not satisfied with their answers, the men bound the fugitives with rope, put them in a wagon, and hauled them away.

When a harried Concklin returned from making arrangements for their next stop, he raced after the Stills. He climbed into their wagon and began untying them in the dark. But then a gun was placed to his head and he was ordered to stop. The dispirited group of fugitives was locked up in the jail in Vincennes. Concklin, still believing that he could rescue them, visited them every day, trying to work out a new plan. He had never met with failure before and was still determined to return Peter Still's family to him.

In the interim, however, a telegram was sent out to various regions in the South with description of the runaways, inquiring if a reward would be offered for their return. Coincidentally, Bernard McKiernon had also sent out a telegram, offering a reward of four hundred dollars for the return of his "property," and another six hun-dred dollars for the "apprehension of the thief; and his delivery in South Florence."

When the abductors learned of the reward, Concklin himself was seized, put in irons, and jailed. A letter sent by Concklin to a friend, asking for bail money, arrived too late to render assistance. McKiernon came to Indiana and identified his slaves, who were then remanded to him without benefit of a formal hearing. He questioned them all. Vina concocted a story in an attempt to protect Concklin, saying that four men had taken them away and delivered them to John H. Miller (Concklin). Concklin denied the existence of the four men, insisting that he had acted alone. This incensed McKiernon, who said that he would see Concklin hanged in Alabama.

In the morning they were all put in a coach and taken to Evansville, Indiana. The prisoners were housed and guarded on the second floor of a private residence. The next morning they were to be sent south onboard the steamboat *Paul Anderson*. Concklin, however, had disappeared overnight. The steamboat was searched, with Vina hoping that he had escaped. It wasn't to be, though. His bludgeoned body was soon found floating in the river, his head fractured and his irons still on. McKiernon, the last person to have been seen with Concklin, insisted that he must have tried to escape and died in the attempt. Concklin's body was buried still bound in chains. There was no further inquiry into his mysterious death.

Back in Philadelphia, word reached Peter Still regarding Concklin's murder and his family's recapture. The brutal manner of Concklin's death when combined with the story of his daring rescue mission did much to bolster support for the Still family's release. An appeal to purchase them back was made to McKiernon, who offered to sell them for the exorbitant sum of five thousand dollars: one thousand dollars per person, and another thousand for his trouble in capturing them from Concklin.

Peter Still began traveling and speaking tirelessly at abolitionist meetings, telling his tragic tale. It took four years to raise the money, but by 1854 he was able to purchase his family's freedom. Vina and his three children were brought to New Jersey where they were warmly welcomed by the extended family. Peter enjoyed fourteen years of freedom with his family until death in 1868.

The Still clan, of which there are now more than three thousand members, continues the tradition set in 1870 of holding family reunions. Family ties, though once severed, still remain strong. Seth Concklin did all he could to reunite Peter Still with his loved ones. It was later written that he was "an abolition society within himself."

THIS SIDE UP

AT THE AGE OF THIRTY-FOUR, AND UPSIDE DOWN in a fetal position, Henry Brown was ready to be born into a new life. It was a tight fit, folding his five-feet-eight, two-hundred-pound form into a tiny wooden crate. The pressure on his head and neck was almost unbearable. His muscles were cramping, and the lack of fresh air was making him dizzy. And yet, it would all be worth it if only he could be released into freedom.

Henry Brown had been born the first time around 1815 on a slave plantation in Louisa County, Virginia. In 1830 when his master had died, he had seen his family split apart, divvied up among the man's heirs. Henry was hired out to work in a tobacco-manufacturing plant in Richmond. He was allowed to keep a portion of his earnings, enabling him to later provide a modest house for his wife and three children. Though he was given preferential treatment, it never made up for the pain of having been separated from his family. Eighteen years later, he was to suffer the pain of separation yet again.

He returned home from the tobacco factory for lunch one day to find his family missing. He was stunned to learn that they had been put on the auction block, sold, and imprisoned until their departure the next day. His wife's owner Mr. Cotrell had previously promised not to sell Henry's wife or their children if Henry had paid him fifty dollars a year. Cotrell broke his promise, however. When Henry begged to buy his own family, he was told, "You can get another wife."

He watched in abject horror as 350 dejected souls filed by, heading toward their new home in North Carolina. Five wagonloads of anguished children wailed for their parents. Henry's eldest child called for him with outstretched arms. His wife of twelve years was led along in a chain gang like an animal, a rope around her neck. Henry stood engulfed in grief—stripped of his manhood, deprived of the ability to provide and care for his family.

Five months later, with little left to lose, Henry decided to make a break for freedom. A bold plan came to him: "The idea suddenly flashed across my mind of shutting myself up in a box, and getting myself conveyed as dry goods to a free state." He only needed to survive the journey.

Henry consulted with Samuel A. Smith, a white storekeeper in Richmond, Virginia, whom he could trust to help execute the plan. Smith traveled to Philadelphia, Pennsylvania, to make the necessary arrangements with the Vigilance Committee, a branch of the Pennsylvania Anti-Slavery Society established to assist runaway slaves. They were informed to look for a box containing human cargo.

John Mattaner, a black carpenter, was asked to construct a box large enough to hold a person but small enough so as not to arouse suspicion of its contents. Another free black, James C. A. Smith, outfitted the crate with baize—a coarse, felt-like, napped fabric—to afford some comfort inside the small compartment. Henry would contort his body into a ball, knees tight against his chest.

Finally, Henry Brown needed a pass from his master to be away from the factory. He intentionally doused his finger with the corrosive acid, oil of vitriol. Injured and temporarily freed from work, he set his plan into action.

On March 29, 1849, Henry gulped a last breath of fresh air and let himself be confined inside his box with nothing more than a few biscuits, a bladder of water, a hat to fan himself, and a gimlet (a screwlike tool used to bore air holes). The box was secured with five hickory hoops by Smith. It was addressed to "William H. Johnson, 131 Arch Street, Philadelphia, Pennsylvania." The words THIS SIDE UP WITH CARE were neatly printed atop the container. Henry's risky, claustrophobic, three-hundred-fifty-mile journey from Richmond to Philadelphia began at 4:00 A.M. The box was put on an open horse cart and taken to the express office. The first leg of the trip was made upside down with no regard for the printed directions. The box was then placed on its side on the baggage car en route to the steamer ship, then loaded upside down again on the steamer itself, where it remained for a period of ninety minutes or so. Henry's head pulsated with pain, and his eyeballs bulged. Surely he was within inches of death.

Voices on deck indicated that people were coming and going. For fear of being discovered, Henry couldn't try to roll the box himself. But then as if in answer to his prayers he heard two men complaining about how they'd been standing for such a length of time. They toppled his box over on its side to make a seat. The unbearable pressure on Henry's head and neck was relieved just in time.

During the remaining overland journey, he was placed right side up, then dropped. He was nearly left behind at the station, but at the last minute the box was loaded onto the luggage train—upside down. Eventually he was placed right side up, and remained that way until his arrival at the Adams Express Office in Philadelphia.

Henry Brown arrived at the depot at 3:00 A.M. He was picked up at 6:00 A.M. To avoid suspicion, E. M. Davis, a mercantile businessman who dealt with the Adams Express Office, sent a hired man to retrieve the box and bring it to the Pennsylvania Anti-Society office where members of the Vigilance Committee awaited his arrival.

On the morning of March 30 several members of the committee gathered inside the office with curtains drawn: J. M. McKim, Professor Cleveland, Lewis Thompson, and William Still—all dedicated abolitionists. The doors were secured, and the gentlemen looked uneasily at each other. They rapped upon the box. "Is all right within?" With the reply, "All right!" the elated men broke open the box and gingerly lifted the cramped Henry Brown to his feet. He immediately fainted away, perhaps from the sudden release of his confinement, the rush of fresh air, or simply the emotion of the moment. He had survived nearly twenty-seven hours inside an incredibly tiny compartment. After the free man, soaked with perspiration, was revived, he quoted a hymn of thanksgiving, "I waited patiently for the Lord . . . and he heard my calling."

News of his bold, imaginative escape was well received, and Henry soon found a new life on the antislavery lecture circuit.

Seven months later Samuel A. Smith, the storekeeper in Richmond, was sentenced to seven years in prison for assisting a similar escape. James C. A. Smith, the free black man who had outfitted the crate, was also convicted, but paid nine hundred dollars for an attorney who was able to acquit him. For a while Henry "Box" Brown and James C. A. Smith toured together on antislavery speaking engagements. After a year of this work, however, Brown came close to being captured and returned to slavery, so he was secreted to England with the aid of workers on the Underground Railroad.

Henry Brown was criticized in the press by antislavery supporters for publicizing his mode of escape. It might have prohibited others from using the same method. Brown, however, insisted that through his notoriety, by educating the public on the evils of slavery and inciting them to take action, he could do more for the antislavery movement than by remaining silent. Sadly, he was never reunited with his family. His life narrative was published both in the United States and in England. Thrilled to be reborn as a free man, newly christened by his harrowing escape, he would go down in history as Henry "Box" Brown.

FREEDOM TRAIN

FOR THE FIRST TIME IN HIS LIFE, nineteen-year-old John Thompson felt free. As the train pulled out of the Alabama train depot, the night wind blew refreshingly cool on his skin. As the train chugged north, all the passengers were treated to a moon-blue landscape under a star-studded sky. Everyone else, however, was inside the train. John Thompson was riding on top of it.

John was done with being a slave. He had been born in Fauquier County, Virginia, in 1838 and had grown up forty miles east, in Alexandria. For as long as he could remember, he had answered to a master. The last time John Thompson had seen any of his siblings was when he was five years old. They had been sold to one place or another, making it impossible for him to have any sense of family.

His earliest memory was of being sold away from his mother Matilda and taken from his home in Virginia to North Carolina. In the years afterward it seemed as if he was sold whenever a master thought there was money to be made off of him. He finally ended up in Huntsville, Alabama, on a cotton plantation belonging to Hezekiah Thompson. While John took on his master's surname, that was all he had in common with the man.

Hezekiah Thompson was a cruel master. The profitability of his plantation crop depended on having his slaves work harder than was humanly possible. Master Thompson was "fond of drinking and carousing, and always ready for a fight or a knock-down." After John Thompson was beaten so severely that his arm was rendered useless for half a week, he decided to make a break for freedom.

For two years he had toiled endlessly in Alabama cotton fields, watching trains pass by. At last he came up with a plan to ride north to freedom. He escaped under the cover of night, making his way to the train depot. When all the ticketed passengers were onboard, the conductor signaled the engineer, and the train slowly lurched out of the station. John hid in some brush by the tracks. When the train began to accelerate, he ran alongside, pulling himself up and scrambling unnoticed to the roof of one of the cars. He lay flat, hanging onto the roof as his heart beat furiously.

John's only plan was to scramble on and off trains, riding at night and hiding during the day. Somehow he had to find out which trains would take him from Alabama back to his childhood home in Alexandria, Virginia, where he hoped he could see his mother again. John had no knowledge of geography. He would have to rely on overhearing people's conversations in the train station. Perhaps he could masquerade as someone's valet, getting luggage; possibly he could hide in the underbrush near the track and listen as the conductors yelled out the train destinations.

For more than six hundred miles and over the course of two weeks, the determined young man fought fear, hunger, and exhaustion as he traveled to Alexandria. Each peaceful night ride through the countryside abruptly ended with the screech of brakes and a billow of steam from the engine. Under the cover of darkness, John would jump from the train and disappear into the brush to wait out the day.

He finally reached Richmond, Virginia, a slave-trading center. He knew that Richmond was not safe, however, because of the many slave chasers in the area. He intended to leave the city, making his way to Alexandria as quickly as possible.

But he was soon spotted and apprehended. Without free papers, he was put in prison and his master sent for. Word reached John Thompson's mother, Matilda, that he was back in the state. She visited him in jail; and while it broke his heart to see her distressed, he reassured her that better days lay ahead.

Hezekiah Thompson came up to claim John, at first intending to take him back to Alabama to "make an example of him." He soon changed his mind, however, and put John up on the auction block.

A Richmond slave trader named Green Murray bought John for $1,300. Murray saw great promise in him, and planned to put him up for resale immediately. But there were no takers at the inflated asking price.

John Thompson was still determined to have his freedom. The train he went looking for the next time, however, was on the Underground Railroad. Many escape routes had their junctions in Virginia, and a well-organized system of "lines" led out of the city. He escaped from Green Murray and made his way back to Alexandria, where he saw his mother once again.

In October of 1857 John Thompson, together with a man named William Cooper, found his way to Philadelphia, to the Pennsylvania Anti-Slavery Society. Their secretary, William Still, was said to assist any fugitive slave who found their office.

William Still listened attentively to John Thompson's story, marveling at his creative mode of escape. The Vigilance Committee then assisted both John Thompson and William Cooper by forwarding them farther north.

Settled in Syracuse, New York, John wrote to his mother, "I hird when I was on the Underground R. Road that the Hounds was on my track but it was no go. I new I was too far out of their Reach where they would never smell my track." He had learned the trade of being a barber and set up shop with a friend. "I am getting $12 per month for what Little work I am Doing." Compared to picking cotton, being a barber surely must not have seemed like hard work.

John Thompson was content and did quite well for two years. However, his former master, Green Murray, had not forgiven him for running away. Someone betrayed John, and he learned just in time that Green Murray was in town, searching for him. Fearing recapture, he immediately took leave of the city and set sail for London, far from the grasp of slaveholders. William Still learned of his arrival across the Atlantic in December of 1860.

There is no record that John Thompson was ever reunited with his mother, or even if he returned to the United States after slavery was abolished in 1865. Perhaps his mother was comforted by a letter he had once written her in which he claimed:

> *I am now a free man Living By the sweet of my own Brow not serving a nother man & giving him all I Earn But what I make is mine and iff one Plase do not sute me I am at Liberty to Leave and go some where elce & can ashore you I think highly of Freedom and would not exchange it for nothing that is offered me for it.*

READ ALL ABOUT IT!

It was the fall of 1850 and James Noble was a man on a mission. With each step he took down the crowded city streets, his anger increased. His destination was the newspaper office of the *Baltimore Sun,* where he intended to place an ad. When the residents of Baltimore, Maryland, picked up their newspapers, they would soon read:

$150 REWARD.
Ran away from the subscriber, on Sunday night, 27th
inst., my NEGRO GIRL, Lear Green, about 18 years
of age, black complexion, round-featured, good-looking
and ordinary size; she had on and with her when she
left, a tan-colored silk bonnet, a dark plaid silk dress, a
light mouslin delaine, also one watered silk cape and
one tan colored cape. I have reason to be confident that
she was persuaded off by a negro man named Wm.
Adams, black, quick spoken, 5 feet 10 inches high, a
large scar on one side of his face, running down in a
ridge by the corner of his mouth, about 4 inches long,
barber by trade, but works mostly about taverns, open-
ing oysters, &c. He has been missing about a week; he

*had been heard to say he was going to marry the above
girl and ship to New York, where it is said his mother
resides. The above reward will be paid if said girl is
taken out of the State of Maryland and delivered to
me; or fifty dollars if taken in the State of Maryland.*

JAMES NOBLE,
No. 153 Broadway, Baltimore.

James Noble had inherited his slave girl, Lear Green, when she
was quite young. Noble and his wife had practically raised her, and
this was how she repaid them? It was preposterous! James Noble was
a respected merchant in town, and he did not appreciate it that his
slave girl had just up and slipped away.

The Nobles had kept Lear Green as busy as possible, but Lear
had apparently still found time to acquaint herself with the free man
William Adams. James Noble later berated himself for not realizing
that Adams was sweet on his Lear.

William Adams and Lear Green had indeed fallen in love. In fact
William had repeatedly proposed to Lear. But Lear had told him the
same thing she had told her own mother: that she would never marry.
Any children born to her while she was a slave would become slaves
themselves, and she wouldn't be able to abide that.

And so William had incentive to seek Lear's freedom. They came
up with an outlandish and dangerous plan. It involved the cooperation of William's mother, a free woman who lived in New York. She
realized that if her son was willing to go to such lengths for Lear
Green, he must truly love her.

Mrs. Adams traveled to Baltimore to enjoy a nice visit with her
son. Afterward she prepared for a journey home aboard the Erricson

line of steamers. An old sailor's chest was arranged with items for the trip home: a pillow, a quilt, some clothes, water, food—and her future daughter-in-law. Mrs. Adams presented her ticket and walked aboard the steamer.

By 1850 the passenger lists for all vessels were being inspected for fugitive slaves. Any ship caught smuggling slaves had to pay five hundred dollars, both the state and to the slave owner.

Though Mrs. Adams was a free woman, discriminatory practices prohibited her from being seated with the white passengers. Blacks were relegated to the open deck of the ship, which was exactly where Mrs. Adam's sailor's chest had been placed.

The steamer pulled away from its dock in Baltimore. Packed tight in her box, Lear Green could feel the rocking of the ship but could not partake in the beautiful, Chesapeake Bay scenery. The ship headed northeast through the Chesapeake and Delaware Canal, then up the Delaware River. Lear Green had begun her suffocating, eighteen hours of confinement. If she were discovered, not only would her own life and safety be in peril but also those of her loved ones. Fortunately, Mrs. Adams was able to secretly lift the lid a few times during the night, checking on Lear's welfare and providing her with some fresh air.

The ship docked in Philadelphia without any of the handlers questioning the contents of the trunk. Still confined, Lear eventually made her way, by means of a jolting carriage ride, to the office of the Anti-Slavery Society in Philadelphia. There William Still, chairman of the Vigilance Committee, opened the trunk, thankful to find Lear Green alive.

Lear remained at the Still residence for several days before being moved to her final destination, a town in southcentral New York where William Adams was waiting.

The young couple was soon married and lived in the town of Elmira, where William's mother resided. They enjoyed three years together. Sadly, Lear Green later died of unknown causes at age twenty-one. If it was any consolation to her grieving husband, her last years were spent in freedom.

William Still so admired Lear Green for her courage and determination to seek freedom at all costs that he had a photo taken of her exiting the trunk and was said to have kept the sailor's chest as a reminder of her valiant efforts. He later said of her that she had "won for herself a strong claim to a high place among the heroic women of the nineteenth century."

THE ART OF PASSING

Ellen nearly panicked when she saw Mr. Cray from Macon, Georgia—a gentleman she had served at Dr. Collins's supper table— coming down the aisle toward her. There were at least ten open seats on the train yet he chose the one next to her. She pulled her hat low and faced the window, hoping he would not see through her disguise. But Mr. Cray was intent on engaging his seatmate in a conversation.

Just the night before, Ellen Craft had been serving supper at the grand Georgia plantation of Dr. and Mrs. Robert Collins. Ellen knew a great deal about the outside world from listening to the conversations that occurred over such meals. Using that knowledge, she had earlier decided to embark on a daring escape with her husband.

When Ellen was a child, and given her light-skinned resemblance to her owner, Major James Smith, she had suffered terribly at the hands of a jealous Mrs. Smith. At age eleven she was given away to the Smiths' daughter as a wedding present. She had been with the Collins family ever since. Now the very color of her skin that had once caused her such misery might allow Ellen and her husband William Craft to escape.

On December 21, 1848, she and William secured passes for the holidays. Ellen donned the disguise of an elderly and ailing gentleman planter. She would travel north with her "slave," William, under the pretense of seeking medical attention in Philadelphia. The key to their success would rest in Ellen's ability to act the part of an infirm Mr. Johnson. If caught, Ellen and William would most likely be separated and sold into hard labor.

Within the four days it took to formulate an escape plan, William collected the components of Mr. Johnson's attire: black boots, trousers, a white shirt, and a long black cloak. Since Mr. Johnson would be suffering from a severe toothache, Ellen's face would be packed with a poultice and her head wrapped in bandages. An ascot scarf under her neck would hide her feminine lines, and her right arm would be put in a sling so as to render it useless in case she was required to write her name. (Ellen was illiterate.) Atop her short cropped hair would be a stovepipe hat, and her eyes would be hidden behind a pair of green spectacles.

At the train station in Macon, Georgia, Mr. William Johnson purchased two tickets to Savannah, one in first class for "himself" and one in the Negro car for his servant. Immediately there was trouble. After they were boarded, Ellen's husband saw his frantic employer out on the platform, searching the windows of the cars. Luckily the train pulled out of the station before he came to where William was seated.

It was the worst kind of luck when Mr. Cray, of all people, boarded the train. Since he had just been to Dr. Collins's house the previous evening, Ellen had spent several hours waiting on him. And now he was sitting next to her. Ellen feigned deafness to avoid being engaged in a lengthy conversation. He at last gave up and directed his conversation to another passenger. Fortunately, he was not going all two hundred miles to Savannah. He departed the train a few stops later.

The Crafts boarded a steamer from Savannah, arriving in Charleston, South Carolina, without incident. Still disguised as William Johnson, Ellen was readily welcomed at one of the finest hotels. But when she attempted to purchase two tickets aboard another steamer for Wilmington, North Carolina, she ran into a skeptical agent. Using a deep voice Ellen explained that as her right arm was impaired, she could not sign the ship's registry. Still, the man remained unconvinced.

Just when the situation looked hopeless, a military officer from Charleston, whom Ellen had met on the first steamer, happened along and vouched for "Mr. Johnson."

After taking the steamer to Wilmington, North Carolina, Ellen and William took a train to Richmond, Virginia, and another to Fredericksburg, Virginia. A steamer took them to Washington, D.C., and from there trains brought them to Baltimore, Maryland, and Philadelphia, Pennsylvania. These were anxious connections, as neither one of them could read.

In addition to several close calls, there was always the fear that news of their escape would be forwarded along by telegraph to major cities and ports. Ellen avoided engaging with passengers and declined all offers of a cigar and drink, for she had no experience with either. She was remonstrated for letting her uppity "nigger" dress too fine and for treating him too kindly. Ellen refused someone's offer to buy William, and at one point quick thinking allowed her to hide her illiteracy. When a passenger offered his calling card, Ellen put it in her pocket without looking at it, avoiding the possibility that she would appear to be reading it upside down.

Ellen and William Craft were almost discovered at their last stop. By law the railroad had to reimburse slave owners if runaways escaped on one of their trains. In Baltimore no one suspected Mr. Johnson of being female or black, but they questioned whether his slave might be a runaway. Consequently, Ellen was asked to show proof of ownership.

Indignant, Ellen said, "I bought tickets in Charleston to pass us through to Philadelphia, and you have no right to detain us here."

Just then the conductor from their last train passed by and verified that the slave had indeed accompanied Mr. Johnson from Washington. Still the officer seemed unconvinced.

As their train was about to pull out of the station the conductor shouted, "All aboard!" The officer began receiving disapproving stares from onlookers for the way he was detaining a sickly gentleman. At last he relented, saying, "Let this gentleman and slave pass." With a nod of thanks, William assisted Ellen hurriedly across the platform to their train to freedom.

Emotionally and physically spent, the fugitives rested fretfully. An exhausted William overslept and was temporarily separated from his "master" when they switched rail cars. For the first time on the thousand-mile trip, William was not there to assist the infirm Mr. Johnson. Ellen grew panicked that William might have been apprehended. Later, upon finding each other, they privately shared a feeling of mutual relief and thanksgiving that their worst fears had not been realized.

On Christmas morning 1848, four days after the start of their journey, Ellen and William Craft reached Philadelphia. The nighttime glow of lights sparkling in the distance meant freedom. On the train William had met a free black man who had told William of a boarding house run by abolitionists. Ellen and William acted on the tip and took a carriage ride to the house. It wasn't until they were alone in their room that Ellen gasped, "Thank God, William, we are safe!" and collapsed weeping into the arms of her husband. They fell on their knees that Christmas morning in prayerful gratitude for a successful escape.

The landlord at the boarding house, delighted to find Mr. Johnson coming down to dinner as Mrs. Craft, notified members of the Philadelphia Anti-Slavery Society's Vigilance Committee. The Vigilance Committee soon forwarded Ellen and William Craft to Boston,

Massachusetts. They were legally married and set themselves up in the carpentry and seamstress business in Boston. Back home in Georgia, however, an irate Dr. and Mrs. Collins heard of the Crafts' escape and were angered and embarrassed to have been outwitted. They sent slave catchers to Boston with warrants for their arrest. The Crafts were nearly apprehended. The Fugitive Slave Act of 1850, which allowed for the capture of fugitive slaves in free states, forced Ellen and William to take refuge overseas.

In December of 1850 the Crafts arrived in Liverpool, England, where they would live for nearly twenty years. They lectured and toured and received an education. Having previously been determined that she would not bear a child under the yoke of slavery, Ellen was very proud that each of their five children was born free in England.

Their biography, *Running a Thousand Miles,* was published in 1860. The Civil War ended, and the Thirteenth Amendment to the U.S. Constitution emancipated all slaves. In 1869 the Crafts and all but one of their children returned to the United States. Two years later, Ellen and William bought a plantation near Savannah, Georgia, not far from where they had formerly lived in bondage. They soon opened The Woodville Cooperative Farm School for black children on their land. In 1890 the Crafts moved to Charleston, South Carolina, where they lived into their seventies. During their nearly fifty years of freedom they created a wealth of opportunities for the next generation.

THE HOUSE ON THE HILL

CLUMPS OF WHITE SNOW FELL FROM THE TREETOPS along the Ohio River. In February 1838 the wet ice of the river was peppered with melting potholes. Given a coming thaw, the river moaned with thunderous cracks as the ice broke up.

In Dover, Kentucky, an anonymous slave mother overheard her master talking to a slave trader. Panic ran through her. Had she just heard right? Did he mean to sell both her and her baby? Or had it been just one of them? Regardless, she was determined to make her escape.

She had heard that there was an abolitionist family in Ripley, Ohio, who had built a house on the highest point above the river, shining a bright lantern out into the night, beckoning slaves to freedom. She planned to go find that light.

As soon as night fell, the woman bundled up her baby and ran out into the cold. After a mile and a half, she made her way to a cabin near the river. She ventured to knock on the stranger's door. Luckily the man took her in. He warned her that it was not a good time to cross the river. With the thaw, nobody had dared to walk on the ice for days.

In the distance, they both heard the baying of bloodhounds. If it was a choice between risking death on the river ice and being separated from her baby, she would risk death. The man understood. He provided her with a wooden plank from his fence to help her on her crossing. He was certain the ice would break and she would need something to hold onto.

With the hounds drawing close, the woman lurched desperately into the icy water. She leapt onto the nearest ice floe, clasping her infant to her breast with one arm and holding the wooden plank in the other. She crawled onto the unsteady sheet of ice. A bone-chilling wind blew across the half-frozen river. Stepping from floe to floe, even those pieces of ice that looked sturdy kept breaking apart beneath her, dropping her into the frigid Ohio River. With each plunge she pushed her baby onto the next frozen chunk and heaved herself up after it, clutching her plank. In the distance she saw a light high up on a hill.

Swimming, crawling, falling, she forced her frozen limbs forward. Mustering every ounce of her remaining strength, she finally waded through the last feet of frigid water and collapsed on the shore.

But her terrifying and courageous flight across the river hadn't gone unnoticed. The notorious slave catcher Chancey Shaw had been watching. He now grabbed her arm, thinking only of the reward for capturing a runaway. The woman looked up into his eyes; her baby let out a cry. Never known to have shown compassion to any fugitive, Chancey Shaw now had a change of heart. Maybe this poor woman and her child had earned their chance for freedom after all. He ushered the half-frozen, exhausted woman through town and pointed her to the house on the hill. Then he disappeared.

The woman looked up the steep hill. One hundred rickety steps could be seen in the moonlight, leading to the red brick house. She saw the beaming lantern and tiredly climbed the steps toward a warm fire.

The Rankin family welcomed the woman and her child, feeding them and giving them dry clothes. The slave woman gratefully rocked back and forth with the baby at her breast. As exhausted as the poor woman was, however, it was too dangerous for her and her baby to stay. They needed to be gone before the sun came up.

Southerners by birth, abolitionists by inclination, the Reverend

John Rankin and his wife Jean had moved away from the slave states of Tennessee and Kentucky to build a home overlooking the Ohio River. They had a clear view of the Kentucky shore across the river. One of Ohio's earliest stations on the Underground Railroad, their light could be seen for miles.

The Rankins had thirteen children and took in another nine. For nearly forty years they gave runaways food, clothing, money, and direction. Assisting fugitives in the dark of night came to be a way of life for the Rankin children. Most typically, one of the boys would take an escaped slave to the town of Red Oak, four miles away, showing them to the home of Reverend James Gilliland. The following day they would be forwarded on to Decatur and Sardinia. Next they might be spirited on to Indiana and the home of Levi Coffin, the "President of the Underground Railroad." From there they would be hurried in and out of various safe houses before finally reaching the safety of Chatham, Canada—more than three hundred miles from the Ohio River.

In 1852 Harriet Beecher Stowe wrote *Uncle Tom's Cabin.* Her legendary character, Eliza Harris, was based on the brave, nameless woman who had crossed the river in 1838. For fear of incriminating the Rankin family—who could suffer fines, imprisonment, and loss of property if identified—the details of the story were changed. Stowe's "Eliza" was a young, light-skinned woman with a four-year-old son, who was taken in by the owners of a white house in Ripley, Ohio. This Eliza knew the man on shore who had apprehended her. She also had a husband and had buried two children before fleeing across the half-frozen Ohio River.

The Ripley First Presbyterian Church, where Reverend John Rankin once preached, maintains a vital congregation to this day. Visitors to the Rankin House in Ripley, Ohio, can climb the reconstructed hundred-step stairway to the top of Liberty Hill, the same hill that led so many slaves to freedom.

I HAVE COME BACK

JOHN RANKIN AND HIS WIFE, JEAN, COULDN'T HAVE been more surprised when, as they were tending their garden in June of 1841, two figures emerged from a nearby wooded lot and strode toward them. The white man was a stranger, maybe Canadian by his dress. But the woman looked vaguely familiar. She was short and heavyset, not quite middle-aged, and dressed as a man in trousers and a waistcoat. Now Rankin recognized her. It was none other than the brave slave woman who had crossed the icy floes of the Ohio River in February of 1838 with her baby. He had never expected to see her again.

John Rankin had learned to be suspicious of surprises. His hilltop house above the Ohio River was a known refuge for runaway slaves, a fact that had antagonized slave catchers from Kentucky for years. He had been mobbed more than twenty times, and there was a bounty of $2,500 for his abduction or assassination.

But this surprise was different. As he learned, the woman had come back from Canada for her grown daughters and grandchildren, slaves on Thomas Davis's farm in Dover, Kentucky. With her was a French Canadian man whom she had hired to help rescue her family. The woman's plan was for the two of them to secret her family across the Ohio River, but they would need the Rankins' help in order to make their way along the Underground Railroad and back to Canada.

Rankin found the woman's rescue plan very risky, and strongly advised against it. Seeing her determination, however, he eventually agreed to assist her. It would take the cooperation of many agents for the undertaking to be successful.

Work was found for the woman in Red Oak, just four miles to the north, so that she could earn her keep while their plan was set into action. Meanwhile her accomplice rowed across the Ohio River and found his way to the woman's enslaved family.

The Canadian had no accent, having lived in many places, and he took care to dress in suitable clothes. He blended in well in Dover. To be near the woman's family, he found a job chopping wood on the Davis farm. He frequented the local taverns and spent time on the riverfront to learn the schedule of the patrollers.

By the first week of August, all was ready. Late on a Friday night, Rankin's sons rowed the woman and the Canadian across the Ohio River. The plan was for the escape to take place the next night.

One of the woman's daughters had seven children and was expecting another. Managing the removal of all these people, as well as their belongings, was going to be a cumbersome trick. Despite their best efforts, the Canadian could see that they would not be able to make it across the river before daylight. The fugitives were forced to hide out on the Kentucky shore on Sunday, hoping to attempt their escape the next night.

Sunday morning Davis awoke to find his slaves missing. He soon helped organize a posse of a dozen men. The Canadian had previously stolen a skiff and rowed it across to the Ohio side, leaving it prominently displayed. The posse crossed the river, spending the entire day searching through the town of Ripley, Ohio, looking for fugitives who ironically hadn't even yet left Kentucky.

A four hundred dollar reward was immediately offered for information on the whereabouts of Davis's slaves. But the machinery of the

Underground Railroad had already begun to turn. The taverns in Ripley, for instance, sold the bounty hunters ale at low prices, hoping to incapacitate them. The Rankin family went to church, knowing that their house would be searched while they were gone.

Around 3:00 A.M. on Monday morning, the Canadian borrowed an abolitionist's skiff and rowed from Ohio to Kentucky, gathering the fugitives and all their possessions. After dropping his passengers off in Ripley, Ohio, the Canadian left immediately. Two other men brought the group up the shore to the home of Kitty and Thomas McCague. The McCagues were known to have slave-owning friends and family in Kentucky, so nobody suspected them of being in collusion with the Underground Railroad.

Rewards were higher for slaves captured across the river in Ohio, and the slave catchers were still out in force. It was important that the fugitives move on immediately. Other members of the underground surfaced to escort the fugitives to the Rankins' house.

Once again the anonymous woman sat in the Rankins' kitchen, just as she had done three years earlier. This time she was surrounded by most of her family, and it was a warm summer evening. However, there was no time to grow comfortable.

From the Rankins' house the former slaves traveled to the Hopkins' farm four miles down the road. Next they were all concealed in a peddler's wagon and were escorted to Hillsboro, Ohio, thirty-five miles to the north. From there they went on to Cleveland, then to Lake Erie, and finally to Canada.

John and Jean Rankin neither saw nor heard from the determined woman and her family again, but were surely glad to hear of their safe arrival in Canada. They were but a few of the two thousand slaves who came through Rankins' house on their way to freedom.

AT WHAT PRICE?

ON APRIL 13, 1848, A SHIP NAMED *Pearl* sailed into Washington, D.C.'s, Seventh Street wharf. Balancing on the bow, feeling the rise and fall of ocean waves, Captain Daniel Drayton surveyed the city. He was intending to pick up the most precious kind of cargo; if all went well, he would live to tell about it.

Two nights later, the citizens of Washington, D.C., were celebrating a revolutionary victory in France. Americans were excited at the idea of democracy spreading around the world, and crowds had gathered for the festivities. There were bonfires, torch-lit processions, and great speeches proclaiming the right to life, liberty, and the pursuit of happiness.

On the fringes of this crowd stood a group of slaves who were not in a celebratory mood. So many aspects of the rally were hypocritical. There was no real liberty for blacks anywhere in America. Domestic animals had more freedom than they did. Fortunately, however, the distractions of this night's celebration made the time ripe for an escape, and New York abolitionist William Chaplin was there to assist the would-be fugitives.

Paul Jennings, Samuel Edmondson, Daniel Bell, and Thomas Ducket had been making escape plans with Chaplin. Jennings, a former presidential slave for the Madisons, was working out the price of his freedom as a servant for Senator Daniel Webster. Samuel

Edmondson was a hired-out slave who had thirteen siblings, mostly enslaved. Daniel Bell was a free black who was involved in litigation to obtain his family's freedom. Fearing that he might lose his case or run out of the money needed for legal fees, he decided to have his family run away. Thomas Ducket, a slave from Maryland, wanted his family free as well.

It was known in some circles that Daniel Drayton, a weathered sea captain from Philadelphia, had recently smuggled a slave woman and six children from Washington, D.C., to Frenchtown, New Jersey. Six weeks later, word had it that he was planning another such excursion along the Delaware River. When William Chaplin had hired Drayton, he'd implied that there would only be "a family or two" that needed safe passage. In reality this was to be the largest escape on the East Coast's Underground Railroad yet.

After the *Pearl* arrived on April 13 those in charge of the escape reviewed the plan. Captain Drayton had charted the sailing vessel from Captain Sayres for one hundred dollars. Drayton would be in charge of the fugitive slaves while Sayres would man the relatively small schooner.

With time running out, the free men and their enslaved families all made preparations to leave. Jennings left his employer, Daniel Webster, a letter of explanation and an apology for his sudden departure. Samuel Edmondson gathered five of his siblings, including two sisters aged fifteen and thirteen. Thomas Ducket's wife and children were ready.

When Captain Drayton learned that a greater number of fugitives were sailing with him than originally planned, he did not object as long as everyone would be aboard by 11:00 P.M.

The *Pearl* was docked under the Potomac's high riverbank. As evening approached on Saturday, April 15, a light rain began to fall. The fugitive passengers crept past the few sparse buildings and open fields on the edge of Washington, D.C. Captain Drayton watched them board his ship, surprised to find his hold overflowing with fugitives. There were more than seventy-six men, women, and children. The number had grown as word of the expedition spread.

Before midnight the fastenings on the *Pearl* were cast off, and the group of hopefuls set sail under the cover of a thin blanket of fog. The path to freedom would take them one hundred miles down the Potomac River, around Point Lookout, and one-hundred-twenty miles up the Chesapeake Bay, through the Delaware Canal to the Delaware River, and on to Frenchtown, New Jersey.

Soon after they set sail, however, the wind died down. Sitting in an ominous calm, nervous tension could be felt among the passengers. Captain Sayres dropped anchor so as not to be carried in the wrong direction by the tide coming in from the Atlantic. A sense of dread hung over all as they waited for the wind to increase. At daybreak a north breeze finally took them around Alexandria, Virginia. As the winds picked up, so did the spirits of the fugitive slaves huddled together in prayer and song in the ship's hold. Around midday they passed a steamer heading in the opposite direction, drawing glares from the passengers on board.

At dusk the *Pearl* reached Point Lookout on the mouth of the Potomac River. A fierce northerly wind prevented them from rounding the point. Captain Sayres, knowing the limits of his vessel, adamantly refused to take her out into open sea. Instead he anchored the *Pearl* in Cornfield Harbor, Maryland, a safe refuge below the point. A sense of foreboding set in. The captains, crew, and passengers bedded down for the night around 9:00 P.M., having no choice but to wait it out. It would be their last rest for a very long while.

Unbeknownst to the passengers and crew of the *Pearl,* they had bigger troubles than the weather: They had been betrayed. A free drayman named Judson Diggs had evidently transported a passenger to the *Pearl,* someone who, as it happened, didn't have money to pay him. Additionally it was said that Diggs's advances toward one of Samuel Edmondson's teens had once been rebuffed. Angered, Diggs turned them all in.

While the *Pearl* was passing Alexandria, Virginia, forty-one different slave owners from Alexandria, Washington, and Georgetown were awakening to discover their slaves missing. The total value of the missing property was estimated at more than $100,000. A posse of thirty-five men was rounded up and directed to the river. Less than twelve hours later, the posse had boarded the steamboat *Salem* and begun their pursuit.

At 2:00 A.M., only one-hundred-forty miles into its two-hundred-twenty-mile voyage, the *Pearl* was overtaken. The shocked passengers and crew were unarmed. The more violent men in the posse wished for an immediate lynching, but cooler heads prevailed. The steamer with the dejected prisoners headed back to the District of Columbia and anchored overnight at Fort Washington. The slave catchers wanted to make an example of the shackled men, women, and children, parading them through the city during the daytime.

It was generally felt that these particular slaves had all been treated very well. Most of the slaveholders were outraged that they would want their freedom. It was decided that most should be sold to the slave-trading firm of Bruin & Hill out of Alexandria. They would be put in a slave pen prior to being sold down south to New Orleans.

The escape attempt of the *Pearl* made national headlines. There was a near riot in the capital when an angry mob insisted that an abolitionist newspaper press be destroyed in retaliation. But antislavery sentiments were also growing as the public came to view the slave owners' claims as hypocritical in light of the celebration for freedom that had occurred just two nights earlier.

Paul Jennings, who had incited many to flee, had never boarded the ship, explaining that his sense of service and loyalty to Senator Webster had kept him from going. He escaped prosecution, but feeling responsible for the fates of the fugitives, he consequently raised the funds to purchase freedom for certain members of Samuel Edmondson's family. During the ordeal both free and enslaved blacks had suffered through the filth and degradation of the slave pens. After three months (and with the help of New York's Anti-Slavery Office), Samuel Edmondson's teenaged sisters were released to their parents. The fifteen-year-old sister died the following year, never having fully recovered from her ordeal. Samuel Edmondson endured a bitter grief for it. A wealthy English cotton merchant purchased Samuel as a butler. Years later, he was able to purchase freedom for himself and his wife and son.

Captain Daniel Drayton was accused of being associated with the abolitionist William L. Chaplin, but he insisted that he had worked alone. Drayton kept silent, as Chaplin allegedly had promised to take care of Drayton's wife and six children if he were ever arrested. Thomas Ducket was implicated in the plot and sold to a Louisiana master. His wife and children were also sold away. He spent the rest of his life appealing to abolitionists to find word of his family's well being.

Captain Drayton and Captain Sayres stood trial for stealing property and assisting fugitives to escape. They were convicted of the latter on appeal and were remanded to prison until they could pay their heavy fines, which would have taken them a lifetime to raise. Four years later President Fillmore granted them an unconditional pardon.

Captain Daniel Drayton never regretted his involvement. He later said, "Nobody in this country will admit for a moment that there can be any such thing as property in a white man. The institution of slavery could not last for a day, if the slaves were all white."

THE DEVIL

LINDSEY PAYNE AND HIS TWO FRIENDS SAT underneath the shade of a large oak tree on May 6, a warm Sunday morning in 1838. Gathered around a fortune-teller's deck of cards, it was Lindsey's turn to cut the deck. As the wizened, old fortune-teller read Lindsey's cards, he arched his eyebrows. Lindsey held his breath. The old man slowly smiled and foretold that Lindsey would escape, become successful, own property, have friends who were both black and white, and one day return to Virginia of his own accord. The news had been better than Lindsey had ever hoped for—he just didn't know it was all to begin so soon.

That very afternoon, eighteen-year-old Lindsey Payne packed a bundle of clothes, some corn cakes and bacon, and took off on a limping run for the James Smith plantation. His life savings of $3.50 jingled in his pocket. Even while hindered by an old childhood leg injury, he needed to cover the two-mile distance in record time. If he was late, he was afraid his two friends, Zip and Lorenzo, would leave without him. News that Zip had been purchased by a Georgia trader had necessitated an immediate escape.

Lindsey Payne lived in Heathsville, Virginia, where he was hired out as a shoemaker. The rest of his family, minus his deceased parents, lived nearby in Northumberland County. He was leaving behind eleven siblings. Realistically he held little hope of ever seeing them again.

Lindsey reached Zip and Lorenzo just in time. The fugitives headed north by boat and then by foot, covering some two-hundred-fifty miles. It felt like an enormous distance, especially for Lindsey with his bad leg. When he was just a young boy, his leg had been crushed by some heavy logs that he was attempting to move. His mother's pleas to Master Langston to seek medical help were ignored and the unattended leg left him crippled.

When it became apparent that the slower-paced Lindsey could not keep up with his two companions, they decided to split up. The two able-bodied men needed to strike out on their own to prevent all three from being captured.

A despondent Lindsey wept to himself at being left behind. His leg had kept him from laboring in the cotton fields, but now it was an enormous disadvantage. During his short life he had already endured a series of cruel masters and mistresses. Once he'd even tried to jump overboard to escape an especially vicious master. He was rescued from drowning only to be beaten badly, even while still regurgitating water. Eventually he had been hired out to learn the trade of a shoemaker which he hoped would help him make a living as a free man.

Lurching on alone, Lindsey fought against despair. There was a chance that the fortune-teller would still be correct. But what happened next terrified him.

At 3:00 A.M. on May 8, the ground shook under Lindsey and a strange thunder rumbled in the distance. He could see nothing in the dark. The horrific noise was coming around the bend. An iron monster reared its ugly head, spouting fire and smoke, screaming furiously on its quick approach. Lindsey had never seen a train before. He scrambled up a steep bank, thinking, "The Devil is about to burn me up. Farewell! Farewell!" With that he passed out.

When he awoke, he was alone in the quiet dark. His imagination began to run away with him. He was sure that he heard the hoof beats of "paddy-rollers" (patrollers, or night watchmen) coming after him. But no, it was only his own heart racing wildly. He resumed his journey.

Around noon he heard the Devil returning, caught on its set of metal tracks, wheels turning and steam pouring forth, choking and wailing. Behind it were a series of wagonlike roofed boxes with rows of white faces in the windows. "Wagons that he carries the souls to hell with," Lindsey thought. Still terrified, he was relieved to see that the Devil was not after black people.

Continuing on, Lindsey eventually arrived at New Castle, Delaware, where he was miraculously reunited with Lorenzo and Zip. The three fugitives planned to take a steamer up the Delaware River to Philadelphia. By law only free blacks could board, but the three runaways must have exuded confidence as they stepped up the gangplank, for no one stopped to question them. They arrived in Philadelphia on Thursday afternoon. Lindsey decided to stay in the United States while Zip and Lorenzo decided to try their luck abroad. This would be the last time that Lindsey would ever see his friends. He would later learn that Lorenzo had died from a cholera outbreak aboard a ship heading to Europe and Zip had died in the West Indies.

In Philadelphia a shoemaker directed Lindsey to a black man named Simpson, an agent on the Underground Railroad. The next day Simpson set Lindsey up with other contacts. Lindsey took the name of the man who had owned the plantation where Zip had lived, christening himself James Lindsey Smith (although he continued to answer to Lindsey).

Friday morning Lindsey was put aboard a steamer to New York City with a letter of introduction to David Ruggles, a black printer and the secretary of the New York Vigilance Committee, part of an Anti-Slavery Society organization that assisted fugitive slaves. Departing from New York three days later, Lindsey took with him two more letters of introduction, one to Mr. Foster in Hartford, Connecticut, and the other to the Reverend Dr. Samuel Osgood, in Springfield, Massachusetts. Lindsey was warmly welcomed upon his arrival in Hartford by Mr. Foster, who took up a collection on his behalf. He then boarded a steamboat for Springfield, Massachusetts, taking with him his next letter of recommendation.

In Massachusetts Reverend Osgood helped Lindsey find employment as a shoemaker. Lindsey said, "It was the first work that I had ever done in the like of a freeman, which gave me the strength to think I was a man with others." The Reverend Osgood also made it possible for Lindsey to attain an education in Wilbraham, Massachusetts, enabling him to run his own business, become a public speaker on the antislavery lecture circuit, and earn a degree as a Methodist minister.

Lindsey married Emeline Minerva Platt in 1842 and settled in Norwich, Connecticut. He eventually bought a home, owned a shoe shop, and educated his four children. Through his preaching and speaking engagements, he did much to convince others of the evils of slavery.

Seven years after settling in Norwich, James Lindsey Smith mistakenly thought that he saw an old master in town. He said, "I had determined never to be taken back alive. Death was preferable to slavery, now that I had tasted the sweets of liberty."

As it turned out, the fortune-teller Lindsey had consulted earlier in his life had been correct on all counts. In 1867 Lindsey returned to Heathsville, Virginia, for a visit. His boat landed at Cone Wharf, the exact spot where he had begun his escape thirty years before. He was reunited with friends, two of his sisters, and a brother.

Many of the wealthy slave owners he had known in Virginia were now poor and hungry. Some of the great plantations had been divided and sold to those who were once enslaved. Lindsey accepted an invitation to dine with his former mistress, a twice-widowed woman whom he knew as Mrs. Sarah Langston. It was she who had done nothing, all those years before, to see that his injured leg received proper attention. She was most interested in the tale of his escape and his new life. In appreciation of her acceptance of him as a free man, Lindsey presented her with a pair of shoes. There had been a time when his former mistress would not walk outside without a slave to hold an umbrella to shade her, but now she was being forced to grow her own subsistence garden under the beating sun.

James Lindsey Smith spent nearly a month visiting the places where he had spent his youth, drinking from springs where his now dispersed family had once gathered. Over the years, he would make repeated visits to Heathsville, often arriving with charitable boxes of clothing and necessities donated by the townspeople of Norwich, Connecticut, where he made his home with his wife and children. As improbable as it seemed, the life of good fortune predicted so many years before was finally his.

A WOLF IN SHEEP'S CLOTHES

THE PETITE WOMAN STARED INTO THE BARREL of a pistol, trying to conceal her terror. It was November of 1846 in Sylvania, Ohio. Defenseless, she and her son found themselves surrounded by several men with drawn guns. Ardent abolitionist Laura Smith Haviland had earlier suspected a trap, and now she was berating herself for ignoring her intuition.

The trouble had all started when Willis and Elsie Hamilton, fugitive slaves who leased land on her farm in Adrian, Michigan, had asked a friend to write a letter to Willis's former master, Deacon Bayliss, inquiring as to the whereabouts of the children they had left behind several years earlier.

Willis Hamilton of Jonesborough, Tennessee, had been set free when his owner decided to manumit all twenty of his slaves in 1843. It wasn't long afterwards that Willis learned that his wife, Elsie, who belonged to a neighboring planter, was going to be sold farther south.

A distraught Willis implored everyone he knew to purchase Elsie for him. A man Dr. John P. Chester bought Elsie for eight hundred dollars, with the understanding that Willis would work off three hundred dollars of her purchase price.

A few months later, however, Elsie got wind of Chester's plan to sell both her and her husband downriver to New Orleans, disregarding the fact that Willis was a free man. Chester planned to catch

Willis off guard, put him in chains next to his wife, and sell them both to a slave trader for a nice profit.

The panicked couple had little time to act. They sought the advice of Deacon Bayliss. He advised the Hamiltons to assume new identities and go north. They would have to leave their daughters behind for now and come back for them later.

The distraught parents were forwarded on the Underground Railroad to a Quaker community in Indiana. After a year they went briefly to Canada and then returned to the states, settling in Michigan. This is where they met Laura Smith Haviland.

In 1846 they wrote a letter to Deacon Bayliss, asking after the whereabouts of their two daughters. They were elated to receive a reply. The deacon reported that the girls were well, but he seemed overly eager to see Willis and Elsie. He wanted to know where they lived and even sent money imploring them to come for a visit. When another letter from Deacon Bayliss arrived, claiming that he had fallen ill on a trip to Toledo, Ohio, and begging them to come see him, Mrs. Haviland refused to write a response, fearing it was a trap.

Instead it was decided that a friend, James Martin, who resembled Willis in appearance, would go see the infirm deacon in Willis's place. Mrs. Haviland and her seventeen-year-old son would accompany Martin.

Upon arriving at the Toledo Hotel, James Martin was told he could see the ailing deacon, and was whisked upstairs by three men. Of course, there was no deacon. But the joke was on the three men, none other than Elsie's old master, Dr. John P. Chester, his son Thomas, and a son-in-law. When they realized that the black man they had just abducted was not Willis Hamilton, they put down their guns and attempted to bribe James Martin into helping them capture the Hamiltons, but to no avail.

Meanwhile, Laura Smith Haviland and her son were growing nervous that James Martin had not returned. She told the proprietor of the hotel that her son had business to discuss with Martin, and threatened to get the law on her side if he did not come down immediately. She also said that she had a message for Deacon Bayliss.

James Martin was brought downstairs and shown to the hotel's dining room to meet with her son. But before Mrs. Haviland could speak with Martin the deacon's doctor took her aside and introduced himself.

"Dr. Taylor," a Toledo physician ostensibly summoned to care for Deacon Bayliss, said that his patient of one week was deteriorating rapidly. Mrs. Haviland told the doctor that the Hamiltons feared a trap and that she had been entrusted with a message for the deacon. She insisted on seeing him even though he supposedly had bilious fever and typhus. Dr. Taylor could see that his plan would go no further until he satisfied Mrs. Haviland's wish.

As soon as she entered the sick chamber, her suspicions were aroused. According to Willis Hamilton, Deacon Bayliss was short and rather portly. The patient in front of her now was thin and over six feet tall. Though his face was covered in bandages, it seemed to be long and angular rather than round. A bin of vomited bile conspicuously placed near his bed looked to be a mixture of coffee grounds and ink with a spattering of spittle. She could feel for herself that the deacon had no temperature and a healthy pulse. Mrs. Haviland acted as if she was quite sure that the poor deacon was indeed on his death bed. She agreed to go back to Michigan and return with the Hamilton family on the next train.

Dr. Taylor replied that the poor deacon didn't have enough time. He recommended sending a messenger by horse. The hotel porter could be hired to ride the thirty-five miles from Toledo, Ohio, to

Adrian, Michigan. In actuality his plan was to have the porter apprehend the Hamiltons until the Chesters could arrive to take them back to Tennessee.

Dr. Taylor requested that Mrs. Haviland be kind enough to write a letter to Willis Hamilton telling him to come immediately. When they left to obtain writing materials, Mrs. Haviland's son crept into the room to warn her that James Martin had found out the men were imposters. She assured her son that she was already quite aware of the ruse.

When Dr. Taylor and the deacon's son-in-law returned, they dictated a letter to her. When they were finished, Mrs. Haviland requested to add a few additional lines of her own, advising Elsie to borrow some traveling clothes for herself and the children. The doctor agreed to the postscript: "Tell Elsie to take for herself the black alpaca dress in the south bed-room, and the two pink gingham aprons and striped flannel dresses in the bureau in the west room for the little girls. To come to Adrian, take the double team farm wagon."

The porter left with the letter. Dr. Taylor thanked Mrs. Haviland on Deacon Bayliss's behalf. After being escorted safely back to the Indiana Hotel, Laura and her son were guarded all night. They figured out that "Dr. Taylor" was actually Elsie's former master, Dr. John P. Chester, and the ill "Deacon Bayliss" was really his son, Thomas K. Chester.

The next morning Laura, her son, and James Martin boarded the 8:00 A.M. train to Adrian, Michigan. The Chesters were also on the train, planning to meet up with the porter they had dispatched to apprehend the Hamiltons. Perhaps the Chesters felt that they had outsmarted Laura Smith Haviland. When the passengers briefly detrained in Sylvania, Ohio, a small farming community ten miles west of Toledo, they approached her with drawn guns, threatening her and calling her names such as "damned nigger stealer."

Refusing to show that she was intimidated, Mrs. Haviland reminded the men that they were no longer in Tennessee. The train conductor came along and took in the scene, then threatened to have the Chesters arrested. The Chesters were clearly outnumbered by a group of irate abolitionists. They fled. Word of the incident spread, and the Sylvania townspeople promised to tear up the track if it were discovered that the Hamiltons were being brought against their will on a southbound train.

Fugitive slaves were often rerouted through Sylvania whenever the Underground Railroad through Toledo was deemed unsafe. The back roads near the Lathrop and Harroun farms were off the beaten track and fugitives were secreted over the ravine between the two houses. Sylvania's abolitionists, who often went so far as to risk hiding fugitives in a concealed room in the Lathrop house, were not about to let the Chesters bring kidnapped fugitive slaves back on the train through their town.

Back home in Michigan, Willis and Elsie Hamilton knew that the letter delivered by the hotel porter was a hoax. Laura Smith Haviland owned neither a black dress nor two pink aprons, and there was no south bedroom in the house or a bureau in the west room. The porter was clearly frustrated by his inability to convince Willis and Elsie to come off with him. Friends who had gathered to advise the Hamiltons made it clear that they would come to their aid if anyone tried to apprehend Willis, Elsie, or their children.

The villainous behavior of the Chesters was exposed. Apparently Dr. John P. Chester was working as a postmaster in Jonesburg, Tennessee, and had intercepted the letter to Deacon Bayliss, who never knew anything about the underhanded scheme.

The Chesters were enraged at being outwitted. They sent a series of threatening letters to Laura Smith Haviland and offered a three thousand dollar reward for her capture, which did nothing to deter her abolitionist works. Within six months of the ordeal, Willis and Elsie Hamilton and their four children had moved to Canada, never having been reunited with the two daughters they'd left in Tennessee.

Three years later, empowered by the Fugitive Slave Act of 1850, the Chesters set out to capture the Hamiltons once again. They went so far as to have a family with four children who resembled the Hamiltons falsely arrested, but they were later released. Dr. John P. Chester was shot through the heart when he attempted to remand a mulatto man into slavery after insisting that his free papers were fake. Chester's son, Thomas, who had impersonated the ill Deacon Bayliss, died a horrible death from yellow fever some months later. On his deathbed, he claimed to see his father waiting to take him to the fires of hell.

Laura Smith Haviland, the petite, Canadian-born Quaker woman whose size belied her strength and resolve, was one of the founders of the first antislavery society in Adrian, Michigan. She was an abolitionist lecturer who helped found the interracial Raisin Institute. She established homes for orphans and served as a nurse in the Civil War. She worked for the Freedman's Aid Bureau, was involved in the temperance movement, and fought for women's right to vote. At the age of thirty-seven she saw five family members die from an erysipelas epidemic, leaving her widowed and in debt with seven children to raise. But even this level of tragedy was not enough to distract her from her goals. During her lifetime she would assist hundreds of slaves in attaining their freedom. Clearly such an accomplished woman of force would not let herself be outwitted by slave catchers.

BAKER'S SPECIAL

MARY "POLLY" JOHNSON WAS THE TALK OF THE TOWN. She was described as a "fair mulatto, always lady-like and pleasant." A thirty-five-year-old widow who had remarried a man nine years her junior, she had been to culinary school in Paris, France, and had just opened a confectionary shop in town. The residents of New Bedford, Massachusetts, were already lining up to taste her iced cakes and ice cream delicacies. The townspeople who frequented her business would have been shocked had they really known what was going on behind the scenes of her bakery.

Nathan Johnson, his wife, Polly, and Polly's children from her first marriage had come to New Bedford in 1819. Nathan had begun working for Charles Morgan, an investor in the whaling industry. Polly had worked as a domestic in Morgan's home. They were both free African-Americans and were proud of the fact that their city had contained no slaves since 1785.

In the mid 1800s New Bedford's major industries, the maritime and whaling trades, provided financial opportunities to blacks. Sea captains sympathetic to runaway slaves often transported them north from southern ports. These escapees usually found ready employment in town. The owners of 21 Seventh Street, Polly and Nathan Johnson (as agents on the Underground Railroad), often assisted New Bedford's fugitives. There were upwards of seven hundred between 1840 and 1860.

In time, and with the assistance of their employer, the Johnsons purchased four properties on Seventh and Spring Streets. After establishing their bakery next door to their home at 23 Seventh Street, they began operating a clandestine operation. The bakery was such a busy place, with people coming and going all day long, who would ever have suspected that the Johnsons were harboring fugitives and forwarding them on to the next station on the Underground Railroad?

Their catering business was set up to serve the city's elite. Polly was well accepted in white society, and her customers enjoyed coming into her shop. Her candies, cakes, and cookies were highly sought after. They catered the marriage receptions for the wealthiest families, threw cake-and-ice-cream parties, and hosted all sorts of celebrations. It was rumored that in 1844 when Wendell Phillips, president of the American Anti-Slavery Society, was asked to come speak in New Bedford, he was enticed by being told that "Polly Johnson will freeze her best ice and ice her best cakes."

Nathan and Polly Johnson were earning themselves a fine reputation and making tidy sums of money while they were at it. And for over thirty years, none of the aristocratic members of New Bedford white society ever realized that the money they spent at the bakery was being used to aid fugitive slaves, nor that slaves were being hidden in the bakery itself.

The Johnsons' block of residential and commercial properties on Seventh Street allowed them the means to support their underground work. As free blacks the Johnsons felt it uncumbent upon them to open their home to any one who was struggling to be free. They came to be recognized as some of the most active black abolitionists in New Bedford.

In 1834 Nathan and Polly Johnson took in five black boarders who had formerly belonged to a Georgian plantation owner. They began educating them, and upon their master's death three years later, the Johnsons took legal action to see that the people were not remanded to slavery by claimants to the man's will.

In September 1838 the Johnsons invited a fugitive to live in their house, a man who would become world-renowned. The young slave, who then went by Frederick Augustus Washington Bailey, had dressed as a sailor and escaped on a train with borrowed free papers. He and his new bride had arrived safely at the Johnsons' doorstep, courtesy of the Underground Railroad. Nathan Johnson lent the newlyweds two dollars to retrieve their luggage, which was being held by the stage driver until they paid for their passage. Then the Johnsons generously invited the destitute couple into their home. Frederick, who took the surname Douglass, found employment refitting ships in New Bedford. He went on to become one of the most significant figures in American history. A famous orator, an abolitionist leader, an advisor to President Abraham Lincoln, Frederick Douglass was perhaps the nineteenth century's most effective American voice for equal rights.

In the 1840s the Johnsons suffered a reversal of fortunes, and Nathan moved to California in 1849, searching for gold. During his twenty-year absence, Polly successfully managed their heavily mortgaged properties and businesses. Their granddaughter, Mary J. Buchanan, a well-educated woman, lived in the house with Polly.

Polly Johnson lived in the house on 21 Seventh Street until her death in 1871 at age eighty-seven. Nathan died in the house at the age of eighty-three. Polly's granddaughter, Mary J. Buchanan, lived in the house until 1891. Upon her death in 1918, she designated that the income from the Seventh Street Johnson properties be used for the general uplift of the black race in New Bedford. The monies from the sale of the properties were donated to the Massachusetts Institute of Technology for the purpose of educating "deserving and ambitious young men of color, of respectable northern parentage, in whatever department of physics they may elect, as being best adapted to their capabilities."

New Bedford was more than an important link on the Underground Railroad. Those who came to New Bedford looking for freedom found hope and opportunity as well. The Johnson house was named a National Historic Landmark for the part it played in local and national history. It is recognized as the first home of the noted abolitionist Frederick Douglass, who was both a passenger and a conductor on the Underground Railroad. Today this same location houses New Bedford Historical Society, an organization dedicated to preserving the rich history of African Americans.

WHERE TO, SIR?

DISGUISED AS A BOY, ANN MARIA WEEMS studied the white pillars and steps of one of the most famous private residences in the world, the White House. She was still surprised to find herself in Washington, D.C. Her escape had initially been hurried, but now she had nothing to do but wait. When her master's slave catchers gave up the chase, she would be taken out of hiding and forwarded on.

Six weeks earlier Ann Maria Weems had huddled miserably in the corner of her master's bedroom, pulling a blanket tight around her shoulders. How foolish she'd been to think that she was receiving a privilege when told she would be sleeping in the main house. She knew now that Master and Mistress Price had been suspicious that she might be planning on running away. Why else would they have made her sleep on their bedroom floor?

According to the law of the day, even though their father was free, all six of the Weems children took on the status of their mother, which placed them in slavery. Thirteen-year-old Ann Maria had already seen three of her brothers sold down South. Other family members had been freed. Fortunately, Jacob Bigelow, an abolitionist lawyer from Washington, D.C., and William Still of Philadelphia's Anti-Slavery Society, had assisted with purchasing the freedom of some of the Weems family.

Ann Maria's mother's freedom had earlier been bought for $1,000, and her sister Catharine's for $1,600. But even though Ann

Maria's master, Charles Price, had been offered $700 to free her, he had refused. After two years it became clear that Ann Maria would have to be taken on the Underground Railroad.

Jacob Bigelow exchanged a series of letters with William Still in Philadelphia. To work out the logistics of the escape plan, he had secret meetings with agents whose true identities he did not know. Washington, D.C. was fifteen miles from Rockville, Maryland, where Ann Maria lived. Jacob Bigelow just needed to get her to the nation's capital, and then he could make arrangements to forward her north.

On Sunday night, September 23, 1855, Ann Maria was secreted away, reportedly with the assistance of two older cousins who were also trying to escape. In early October she arrived in Washington, D.C. Jacob Bigelow was a respected lawyer with offices on East and Seventh Streets. No one suspected that he was an agent on the Underground Railroad, running a route through Montgomery County, Maryland.

Using the name William Penn, Bigelow wrote in code to William Still about a "small package" and said, "Merchandize shall be delivered" to William Wright, an underground agent in York Springs, Pennsylvania.

While plans were being finalized, slave catchers came to D.C. looking for Ann Maria Weems. Her master, Charles Price, had offered a five hundred dollar reward for her capture, but no fifteen-year-old slave girl fitting her description could be found. Nobody, however, was looking for a fifteen-year-old boy.

After six weeks of hiding Ann Maria in the nation's capital, "the storm had passed," and Bigelow felt safer conducting her to the next stop. Disguised as "Joe Wright," she donned a boy's black pants and white shirt, a vest, jacket, and neat bow tie. Her hair was cropped, and a cap pulled down low to hide some facial freckles. Having been schooled as to how a carriage driver should talk and act, young Joe looked the perfect part of a gentleman's coachman.

Arrangements were made for Ann Maria to travel with "Dr. H." in late November. Bigelow did not know the man's real name. On the appointed day the esteemed Jacob Bigelow, Esq., and his young coachman set out. They had decided to rendezvous in a very public place. The city was abuzz with people coming in and out of the Treasury building and the State, War, and Navy buildings on the brisk fall afternoon. It did not seem out of the ordinary that an unattended horse and buggy should be tied up in front of the White House on Pennsylvania Avenue.

Dr. H. confidently climbed inside the carriage. At that moment Mr. Bigelow and the young coachman walked up. Joe Wright tipped his cap to Dr. H. while the two older gentlemen shook hands. Without further ado the young driver unhitched the horses from the hitching post, climbed into the seat, took the reins, and drove off. Jacob Bigelow's work was done.

The good Dr. H. took the reins when they were alone on the country roads and put his young charge at ease. They would travel together through several counties in Maryland, along the eastern Pennsylvania border, and on to Philadelphia. It would be necessary to find lodging for a night. Dr. H. told "Joe" that he would look up an old acquaintance and inquire if they could spend the evening.

Dr. H.'s friends were quite glad to see him and insisted that they accommodate him overnight. When asked why he had come this way after being absent so long, Dr. H. explained that he had not been well. His own physician had suggested that a good drive in the country air might be beneficial to his health.

Ann Maria listened from the kitchen as the adults visited in the parlor. Dr. H. put on all sorts of airs and talked on a variety of subjects, ready to agree heartily with his friends' proslavery sentiments. Ann Maria knew her place and acted as she had been instructed.

At bedtime Dr. H. suggested his boy remain with him during the night, as his vertigo caused dizzy spells. The friends found the request understandable and made arrangements. In actuality Dr. H. felt safer if Ann Maria was not out of his sight during the evening. Slave catchers may have followed them, or her disguise as a boy might be found out if she was out of his sight. Once again Ann Maria found herself with a blanket on the floor while her "master" slept nearby.

By morning the good doctor was on his way, with his devoted coachman at the reins. Ann Maria must have been overjoyed when she crossed into the free state of Pennsylvania. They arrived at the home of William Still in Philadelphia at 4:00 P.M. on November 25—Thanksgiving Day.

Though William Still was expecting their arrival, he was not at home. Dr. H. greeted Mrs. Still and told her that he was most anxious to hurry home. He stated, "I wish to leave this young lad with you a short while, and I will call and see further about him." With no goodbyes Dr. H. left and was never seen again.

Joe Wright sat nervously in the kitchen in the company of Mrs. Still, a hired girl, and a female runaway slave. When William Still returned home, he was elated to see the disguised coach girl and greeted her accordingly: "I suppose you are the person that the doctor went to Washington after, are you not?" But the young coachman insisted that his name was Joe Wright from York, Pennsylvania, and that he was a servant traveling with the doctor. William Still replied, "The doctor went expressly to Washington after a young girl, who was to be brought away dressed up as a boy, and I took you to be the person."

The boy's insistence that he was not that person perplexed William Still, who did not find out the reason for the denial until the two were alone. Ann Maria had been under strict orders not to reveal her true identity to anyone but Mr. Still. In the presence of Mrs. Still and the others, Ann Maria Weems had been taking every precaution not to give herself away.

After several days' rest in Philadelphia, Ann Maria, still disguised as Joe Wright, continued her journey by coach to New York City. Lewis Tappan, an elderly abolitionist in Brooklyn, paid three hundred dollars for her transport.

In New York, Reverend Freeman, a black minister, was to accompany Ann Maria on the remainder of the journey. The two boarded a train from New York City to Canada. The long train trip was fraught with worry, as there was now a sizable reward being offered for Charles Price's runaway slave. It wasn't until they passed into Canada that Ann Maria felt safe.

In December of 1855, a full two months and four hundred miles from where she had started, Ann Maria Weems arrived in Chatham, Canada. The fourth and final phase of her journey took her on a twenty-mile carriage ride to the home of her aunt and uncle, the Bradleys in Dresden.

Ann Maria Weems was educated at the reputable Buxton Mission School in the Elgin Settlement, a cooperative colony for refugees in Canada. By 1858 all six of the children in the Weems family had finally won their freedom. In 1861, when Ann Maria was twenty-one years old, her parents and two youngest siblings moved to Canada for a period of time. After 1861, however, all records of Ann Maria Weems's life are lost to time. It is hoped that this very brave young lady went on to enjoy many years of freedom.

FOLLOW THE DRINKING GOURD

BARNEY TURNED AND LOOKED AT HIS REFLECTION in the mirror. There stood the slight form of a twenty-five-year-old woman dressed in a blue gown and cape with long white gloves. Her head was adorned with a frilly bonnet. Lace encircled her face. Her eyes, a combination of hazel and blue, peered out from a complexion of white and pink greasepaint. The transformation was unbelievable, but Barney couldn't help but worry what kind of punishment he might receive if he were caught impersonating a white woman.

Barney and his mother, Phoebe, had once lived as slaves on the Virginia plantation of his biological father, Master Charles S. Darlington. The fact that Barney's eyes and skin were lighter was now a great advantage, as it allowed him to disappear into his disguise. His mother's dream for Barney had always been for him to run away, get an education, and make a life for himself. In 1836 she drowned while trying to find an escape route for him. Barney was then sold to Master Bartlett. He got a partial education by listening to his new master read aloud on their long journeys to market. After Barney was sold to an owner near Columbus, Georgia, he had a chance to learn more. Mistress Fenstanton took a liking to him and encouraged Barney to continue learning to read and write by secretly allowing him the use of Master Fenstanton's library. His education improved a great deal in his seven years with the Fenstantons.

When he was twenty-four years old, Barney was hired out to work on a Mississippi steamboat, the *Magnolia Blossom.* The expansive riverboat was something to behold, with its glass-enclosed deck, giant paddle wheel, and powerful steam engine. It traveled from Louisville, Kentucky, down the Ohio River to the Mississippi, all the way to New Orleans then back again. Barney saw more sights than he had ever imagined possible. He was also able to witness a variety of entertainments.

While working on the *Magnolia Blossom,* Barney had been befriended by a British Shakespearean actor named J. Anthony Preston. One of Barney's jobs was to look after the actor's dressing room. Preston realized that Barney had great potential and thought that he would do well if he ever escaped. He explained to Barney that there were people who opposed slavery, and he gave Barney northern newspapers to read. When Barney shared his wish to be free, Preston said he would help him escape. Preston taught Barney how fugitive slaves used the Big Dipper, referred to as the Drinking Gourd, to find the North Star and thus guide them to Canada. Barney learned about the Underground Railroad, and Preston told him that people who wore red handkerchiefs were often friends of the enslaved and would help show him the way to freedom. He would be taught code words that would help him meet up with his contacts. Though Preston was not directly involved with the Underground Railroad, he was sure that he could set up Barney with people who were.

After a year or so, Master Fenstanton decided that Barney's time on the *Magnolia Blossom* was over. He wanted Barney back on the plantation in Georgia. From talking with J. Anthony Preston, Barney realized that he would never have a better chance to escape than when the riverboat was docked on the Mississippi River next to a free state. It was Preston who arrived at the idea of dressing Barney up as a woman.

Preston awoke Barney, disguised as Miss Cora May, from the trance he had fallen into while staring at himself in the dressing room mirror. The *Magnolia Blossom* had docked at Quincy, Illinois, and it was time to depart. As they left the dressing room, Mr. Preston engaged in a lively conversation with the charming young Miss Cora May, who held his arm and hung on his every word.

It was a mass of noise and confusion on the deck of the *Magnolia Blossom*. Bells rang above the splashing water from the great paddle wheel. Deckhands yelled directions as they unloaded crates. Outwardly calm but inwardly terrified, Barney sashayed down the gangplank on the arm of Mr. Preston. His heart briefly stopped when the ship's captain came toward them, but the man only nodded good day and then passed by.

Preston found a carriage for hire, gave the password to the driver, and assisted Miss Cora May inside. Tears of joy would have ruined his makeup, so Barney composed himself as the carriage took him away to the Underground Railroad.

His first stop was a barn. Inside, Barney was given a chance to clean up and put on men's clothing. He hid in the hayloft until evening, at which time he was put in a wagon and covered with straw. He traveled until daybreak, then once again was hidden in a barn loft. The plan was to forward him to Peoria, Illinois, but word had it that slave hunters and their bloodhounds were scouring the area, looking for runaways.

To avoid capture, Barney's conductor backtracked. While this seemed counterproductive, Barney realized that he had no other choice but to trust those who were helping him. Barney was given falsified papers and put on a boat going south on the Illinois River. He worked on the boat as directed, loading and unloading crates. After several days a farmhand wearing a red handkerchief came by to hire some men. He asked Barney in code, "Who's your friend?"

Barney replied, "The North Star is my friend," and the contact took him on.

Barney was informed that his escape from the *Magnolia Blossom* had been discovered and that he needed to be forwarded north along an alternate route. He was pointed to a town and told to knock on the door of a certain doctor's office. He was then whisked to a nearby cellar, where he spent the day. That evening he was hidden in a wagon that took him to a funeral home. Barney was put inside a casket with small air holes and driven forty miles. He was let out, given some cursory directions and signposts, and told that he was to follow the Drinking Gourd to a town called Vandalia.

Barney traveled at night and hid during the day in fields or woods. When he heard dogs barking in the distance, his heart raced, and the hair stood up on his neck. At one point he narrowly escaped a group of patrollers. Muddy, thirsty, hungry, and exhausted, he braved all sorts of weather and walked a seemingly endless number of miles. At times he found churches that offered him food and at other times he went hungry. But always, he kept the North Star as his compass.

In what would become Kankakee, Illinois, Barney searched for a certain church he'd been told about. He found his next contact and was hidden in the church's belfry and given food. A few days later he was transported out of town in the false bottom of a vegetable wagon.

Barney completed his circuitous route to freedom and arrived safely in Chicago, Illinois, having been delivered to a livery stable. He became friends with the owner of the livery, H. O. Wagoner, and began working with him on the Underground Railroad, assisting many fugitive slaves. In 1849 at the age of twenty-seven, he married Wagoner's sister-in-law, Julia Lyoni. She had told Barney to take a surname and suggested Lancelot Ford, after a popular railroad steam engine of the day.

Barney L. Ford was destined for success. In 1851 he and his wife set out for the California gold fields by ship. When they reached Central America, Barney decided to stay in Nicaragua and build a hotel and restaurant. The enterprise was very successful.

Barney was then lured west by the Pike's Peak Gold Rush in 1860. At age thirty-eight he went to Colorado to try his luck. After he was cheated out of his mining profits by a claim jumper, Barney brought his family to Denver and began a career as a barber and small restaurateur. His business and much of Denver were burned in the great fire of 1863, but Barney borrowed money to rebuild. With his profits he eventually built several restaurants and grand hotels in Denver and Cheyenne, Wyoming. He became a prominent restaurateur, caterer, and hotelier whose businesses were frequented by dignitaries and presidents. The well-respected tycoon had ended up being one of Colorado's wealthiest men.

Barney Ford achieved a level of social status and prominence that he never could have imagined as a child. When he had walked down the plank to freedom in 1847, he had felt very much alone in the world. Yet 145 years later, in 1992, Barney L. Ford was listed as one of the one hundred greatest Coloradoans. Eventually known as the "Black Baron of Colorado," he was posthumously inducted in the Colorado Business Hall of Fame.

THE ELEVENTH HOUR

SAMUEL D. BURRIS WAS STRIPPED OF HIS CLOTHES and dragged nearly naked to the slave auction block in Dover, Delaware. Poked and prodded by potential buyers, the slave owners felt his muscles, checked his head for lice, looked at his back to see if he had been whipped, and probed in his mouth to inspect his teeth. His worst nightmares were coming true.

Samuel D. Burris was a free, educated black man. He had been born in Willow Grove, Delaware, in 1808. A black person in the state of Delaware was considered free unless proven otherwise, but ads offering rewards for runaway slaves appeared frequently in newspapers, and sometimes free black people were abducted because they resembled descriptions of runaways. They were kidnapped and taken back to slave states without the benefit of a trial.

The free state of Delaware bordered Maryland (a slave state) on the west, and Pennsylvania (a free state) on the north. As an adult Burris had moved with his family to Philadelphia where there was a vibrant community of abolitionists. He partnered with Thomas Garrett of Wilmington, Delaware, and John Hunn, a Maryland Quaker, in working on a system of secreting fugitive slaves to Canada. In time Burris came to be recognized as an agent of the Underground Railroad. He would often go deep into Maryland to conduct a group of fugitives northward, stopping at various stations along the Underground Railroad. Burris's belief in what he did and his success as both an agent and conductor may have allowed him to think that he was invincible.

Proponents of slavery were suspicious of Samuel Burris, and no doubt kept a watchful eye on him. In 1848 he was apprehended in Dover, Delaware, with a band of runaway slaves, and was thrown into the Dover jail. When news of his capture reached John Hunn and Thomas Garrett, they contacted the Anti-Slavery Society in Philadelphia. Though the members of the Anti-Slavery Society had not always sanctioned Burris's actions, they were well aware of his services in bringing slaves to freedom. They set out to do what they could for him.

Burris sat in prison for months while he awaited trial. Meanwhile, preparation for a legal battle was moving forward just one hundred yards away in the state capitol. James M. McKim of the Anti-Slavery Executive Committee took particular interest in Burris's case. McKim and his office, along with John Hunn and Thomas Garrett, implored the governor to intervene on Burris's behalf. The governor turned a deaf ear.

At Burris's trial it was determined that legislation enacted in 1837 should be upheld. The law clearly stated that any free black person convicted of assisting fugitive slaves would be sold into slavery himself for a period of time determined by the court. The judge gave Burris a sentence of seven years of servitude. A shocked and dejected Burris was led out of the courtroom. There would be no appeal.

In September of 1848 Burris was led down the steps of Delaware's State House to Dover's town center. He was made to stand with the very people he had risked his life to save. Dejected and demoralized, no doubt stunned by man's inhumanity to man, he was pushed roughly to the forefront. The auctioneer began to enumerate his fine physical attributes. Burris caught the eye of his friend John Hunn among the group of spectators, and Hunn's sympathetic countenance said it all. There was absolutely nothing he could do.

Two slave traders from Baltimore were bidding against each other for Samuel Burris. Another trader, a southern gentleman new to the area, seemed to have a particular interest in him. The man postured as if he had a great deal of money to spend. One of the Baltimore dealers was in the lead, with a bid of $500. The southern buyer upped the ante to $600, giving the impression that he would be increasing the bid in increments of $100. The dealers from Baltimore hesitated. After the slightest pause the auctioneer cried, "Sold!" and pounded his gavel. The sound reverberated in Burris's ears.

John Hunn watched dejectedly as Burris was led off the block. Those who had come to witness Burris's punishment for breaking the law had smug looks on their faces. Hunn only shook his head and sadly walked away.

But the southern buyer who had purchased Burris seemed indifferent. He picked up his bill of sale and led his new property away. When they were out of sight of the slaveholders, his "owner" whispered into Burris's ear, "You have been bought with abolition gold." It must have been hard for Burris to believe. It had all been a ruse.

The "slave owner" who bought him was none other than Isaac S. Flint, an avid abolitionist from Wilmington, Delaware. James McKim from Philadelphia's Anti-Slavery Society could not dare let John Hunn or Thomas Garrett pose as the slave trader, for fear of being recognized. Instead someone with a low profile was chosen. McKim had raised the necessary funds to buy Burris right out from under the nose of the slave traders. Under an assumed name, Flint had been studying the Baltimore slave traders until he could mimic them perfectly. Fortunately the bidding had stopped when it did; if the amount had been too high, Burris's fate would have been sealed.

In a strange reversal of roles, Samuel D. Burris was now a passenger on the same Underground Railroad he had previously supported. He was conducted to Philadelphia and reunited with his family.

That same year, John Hunn and Thomas Garrett were tried and fined for assisting other fugitives. It nearly bankrupted the men, but they continued their work for freedom's cause.

After a few years in Philadelphia, Burris took his family to California in 1852. He kept abreast of the Underground Railroad's activities back East, however, and did what he could to help. He also assisted former slaves who had come to California looking for a better life. After the Civil War, when there was a particular need to assist the freed slaves seeking refuge in Washington, D.C., Burris contacted the black churches in San Francisco to raise funds for the cause. In 1869 he died at the age of sixty-one, eulogized as a man who had devoted his entire life to the fighting of injustice.

THE LETTER OF THE LAW

ON THE EVENING OF JUNE 1, 1848, TWENTY-TWO-YEAR-OLD John Walker snuck back onto Ruel Daggs's farm. He had escaped several months earlier and was returning now for his wife, Mary, and their baby. Several other slaves decided to run away with John Walker that night: Sam Fulcher, his wife, Dorcas, and their three-year-old son; their eighteen-year-old daughter Julia Fulcher; ten-year-old Martha; and a young boy named William. The fugitives had no idea that they were soon to become embroiled in a prolonged federal court case—the first of its kind dealing with the Underground Railroad in Iowa.

A slave catcher named Sam Slaughter had been following muddy wagon wheel ruts for hours and was now convinced that he was on the heels of the fugitives. When he spotted a wagon with a covered top beside a creek, he thought his chase was over.

The wagon was driven by Jonathan Frazier, son of the leader of the Anti-Slavery Friends in Iowa, and two of his friends. Instead of finding fugitive slaves, Slaughter was sorely disappointed to find only three white men who claimed they were returning from a fishing trip near Des Moines. Slaughter said he was only looking for two escaped horses. They studied each other with distrust but agreed to ride on together toward the nearby town of Salem, Iowa. John and Mary Walker and the other fugitive slaves hidden off the road all held their breath.

Ruel Daggs's farm was nestled in the gently rolling hills of northeastern Missouri. It was less than thirty miles from the free state of Iowa, which may have been why Daggs was now missing nine of his sixteen slaves. Daggs had a reputation as an honest, fair man who treated his slaves well, but he supposed that they might have gotten wind of the fact that he was thinking of selling them south.

The band of hopeful fugitives headed first to the home of Richard Leggen. They took refuge there knowing that slave catchers were in hot pursuit. Seventy-three-year-old Ruel Daggs, who suffered from diabetes, had put his sons in charge of regaining his property.

Daggs's son William and a neighbor named James McClure went first to Salem, Iowa, which was known as a regional center of abolitionist activity. William Daggs hired a local man named Sam Slaughter to assist McClure in the search.

Meanwhile the slaves were taken from Leggen's house to the Des Moines River, swollen from the recent rains. They managed a hazardous crossing on a crude raft, just below Farmington in southeastern Iowa. The deluge continued all day Saturday, while the men, women, and children took cover under trees along the shore, awaiting transportation. They were then taken to Salem, Iowa, twenty-five miles north of the Missouri–Iowa border.

When they were less than a mile south of Salem, Iowa, Sam Slaughter came up on the wagon, nearly catching the fugitives. Fortunately the three young men driving the wagon had noticed a rider on a fast horse approaching. They wisely pulled off to give the fugitives a chance to hide.

Slaughter later joined up with McClure, staying overnight in a local hotel in Salem. Slaughter was convinced that the slaves must be nearby. Why else had that wagon on the road increased its speed?

On Sunday morning Slaughter and McClure widened their

search, eventually finding nine slaves hidden about two hundred yards off the road along Little Red Cedar Creek. John and Mary Walker, Sam and Dorcas Fulcher, Julia, Martha, William, and the two small children had been on the run for three days.

The leader, John Walker, resisted recapture but was finally restrained. It was such a large group of slaves, the slave catchers decided they needed assistance. While McClure guarded the captives, Slaughter took off to secure additional hired hands to manage their return to Missouri.

By the time that Slaughter returned, twelve abolitionists—including Elihu and Thomas Clarkson Frazier, and Henry Johnson—had surrounded McClure and the slaves. One of them said that he would "wade in Missouri blood" before the men, women, and children were hauled away. No one was going anywhere without seeing an officer of the law first.

They walked to Salem to see the justice of the peace, Nelson Gibbs. An unruly crowd of onlookers gathered. The confusion made it difficult for Slaughter to keep track of the slaves. John Walker slipped away in the crowd, and Slaughter soon feared that he would lose them all. Not wanting anyone to get hurt, Sam Fulcher promised the slave catchers that the others would never leave without him. Slaughter trusted his word and just kept an eye on Fulcher and his three-year-old son.

Justice Gibbs's office in Salem was in the Henderson Lewelling house, originally built as a station on the Underground Railroad, complete with trapdoors leading to three secret rooms. The proceedings were soon moved to the Anti-Slavery Friends' meeting house, as the Lewelling house could not accommodate the crowd of nearly one hundred proslavery and abolitionist townsfolk who had gathered. Both groups of people were loudly voicing their opinions as to how the situation should be handled.

Attorneys were appointed for the slaves. In just a few hours, Justice Nelson Gibbs ruled against the slave catchers. Not only did Slaughter and McClure not have arrest warrants, they also couldn't personally identify the slaves.

Slaughter and McClure were acting as agents for Daggs by verbal agreement only. They had no written documentation proving they were acting on his behalf. Justice Gibbs, who was an antislavery magistrate, conducted an informal inquiry and decided his court did not hold jurisdiction. He declared that the fugitives were free to go. Sam Fulcher carried his three-year-old son to a horse that was offered to them and rode away. The rest of the slaves were assisted on their way to freedom. McClure and Slaughter vowed revenge for being robbed of their captives.

A few days later the two slave catchers, along with over one hundred armed Missourians, returned to Salem. At the time the city could only boast a population of about five hundred people. The slave catchers set up roadblocks going out of town and began to search for Ruel Daggs's slaves. While they did not search the homes of the townspeople without permission, they coerced the homeowners with their rough language.

Unsuccessful in their search, McClure and Slaughter enlisted the help of a local proslavery man who identified all those who had been involved in assisting the slaves to escape. The Missourians arrested over ten men using blank warrants issued by a constable in another town. Some of the men included Elihu Frazier and Thomas Clarkson Frazier, who had prevented the slave catchers from initially leaving town with the slaves, Thomas Frazier's son, Jonathan, who had driven the slaves in the wagon, and John H. Pickering, whose horses had pulled the wagon. All were held captive in a hotel by the Missourians. A Henry County sheriff arranged for their release after they signed a recognizance to appear at a hearing in federal district court.

The angry Missourians threatened to burn the town and start lynching abolitionists if they did not find the fugitives.

Antislavery supporters from Denmark, twenty miles southeast of Salem, had come to answer the Missouri mob's threats and to assure peace. When these reserves returned home, they took Sam Fulcher and his young son (whom some townspeople in Salem had been harboring) with them. John Walker, who had instigated the escape from Daggs's farm, made it to freedom in Canada with his wife and baby.

Four of the nine slaves were eventually recaptured by the Missourians and returned to Ruel Daggs: Sam Fulcher's wife, Dorcas, their daughter, Julia, and the two children, William and Mary.

Ruel Daggs sought compensation for the loss of service of his nine slaves. He brought suit against nineteen men in a U.S. district court in Iowa in September of 1848. The case of *Daggs v. Frazier, et al.,* dragged on for two years.

According to the Fugitive Slave Act of 1793, the U.S. Constitution recognized the institution of slavery and upheld the right of the slave owner to reclaim his property from another state. The jury took two hours to find six of the defendants in violation of the Constitution, maintaining that the men had no right to release another man's property and that no moral law was to stand above the Constitution. Judge John J. Dyer overruled the jury and found just five of the defendants guilty on two counts of harboring and concealing those they knew to be slaves.

The men were fined $2,900, presumably the combined market value and loss of services assigned to the five fugitive slaves who had escaped. There is no record that Ruel Daggs ever received any of the money after the prolonged court battle. All but one of the men charged had previously transferred their assets to trusted individuals.

NOT MY CHILD

THE YOUNG MOTHER LOOKED DOWN INTO THE PLEADING and terrified eyes of her little ones. They clutched the folds of her skirt, holding on for dear life as chaos broke out all around them. Glass was breaking, doors were being battered down, and gunshots were going off. There was no escape. Before she knew it, Margaret Garner had done the unthinkable. How had everything gone so wrong?

Margaret Garner and her family and friends had been planning to make a run for freedom for some time. She was part of a group of seventeen slaves owned by Archibald K. Gaines and John Marshall of Boone County, Kentucky, not far from the free soil of Ohio. Their plan was to wait until winter and then head to the Ohio River and walk across the frozen water. Margaret Garner, who may have been expecting again, and her husband, Robert, were accompanied by their four children, two boys and two girls, as well as her elderly in-laws Simon and Mary Garner. The youngest was a daughter just several months old.

It was a freezing cold night on January 27, 1856, when the group set out. They stole two horses and a sled from one of the master's barns and quietly led the horses past the slave quarters. All seventeen bundled up as best they could and climbed into the sled. Horses' hooves clopped and sled runners whispered over snow. If caught, they would be charged not only with horse stealing but with absconding with their owner's other property—the sled and themselves.

It was not yet dawn when they arrived at Covington, Kentucky, across from an area called Western Row on the Ohio River. The group tied up the horses and slipped over the frozen river to Ohio. To avoid attracting attention, they decided to disperse into the streets of Cincinnati. With hoods and scarves covering their faces and heads bent low out of the blustery winds, the two groups of slaves separated and went their own way.

The nine slaves who had belonged to John Marshall went uptown, seeking out safe houses. They would stay the night in Cincinnati before being safely forwarded along the Underground Railroad to Canada.

The eight slaves that made up the Garner family asked for directions to the home of Elijah Kite, a free black kinsman who lived a few miles from the river. They found a safe haven there and warmed themselves by the fire as they discussed the next course of action. They knew full well that Gaines and Marshall were already pursuing them.

After feeding the Garners, Elijah Kite went to the office of Levi Coffin, just a half-mile away, seeking advice. Coffin, the well-known "president" of the Underground Railroad, told Kite to move the Garners immediately to Mill Creek, a black community outside of the city. From Mill Creek, arrangements would be made to move them along the Underground Railroad.

Elijah Kite returned with the good news, only to find his house surrounded by a posse of men, including Archibald Gaines, John Marshall, and a U.S. marshal and his deputy. Gaines demanded that the slaves surrender. All hopes of escape were seemingly dashed. It had only taken a few hours for Gaines and Marshall to discover that their slaves were missing, and they had traced their path in the snow to Cincinnati. A few more inquiries directed them to Kite's home.

Margaret Garner had come so close to setting her four children free. She wasn't going to give up her hopes so easily. She and the other adults barred the doors and windows, grabbed knives, clubs, and guns, and vowed to die fighting rather than be taken back to slavery.

One of the windows shattered, spraying glass across the floor. The screams of children pierced the air. There was no time to think, only act. Outside in the yard, Deputy Marshall John Patterson was grazed by a bullet fired from inside the house. The door was rammed and nearly broken off its hinges. In the chaos Margaret Garner declared that she would rather kill her children and herself than return to slavery. As the door broke down, her husband shot off his pistol, wounding one of the men before he himself was overpowered. In the noise and confusion, Margaret looked down at her beautiful three-year-old daughter, Mary. The little child would now have to endure the same degradation and horrors of slavery that she had. She wanted to save her from the same agony.

Before she quite knew what she was doing, Margaret Garner had taken a knife and slit the throat of her dear daughter. In the confusion of the fighting around her, she then attempted to take a shovel and beat her four-year-old and six-year-old sons over the head. She would save them from the evils of slavery as well.

Margaret's elderly mother-in-law witnessed the horrible scene but did not intervene, perhaps understanding that she might have done the same under similar circumstances. Elijah Kite's wife disarmed Margaret, and one of the men overpowered her before she could take her own life. The distraught young mother fell to the floor, sobbing. She cried that "she would rather kill every one of her children than have them taken back across the river." Margaret Garner's daughter soon died. Her two sons, while bloody, were without serious injury. The infant was bruised in the melee but survived.

The Garner family was apprehended and brought before a U.S. District Court in Cincinnati. They offered barely audible answers to a barrage of questions. When asked about an old scar across the side of her face, Margaret answered dully, "White man struck me." When it was suggested that she had gone insane in killing her own daughter, Margaret answered quite clearly, "No, I was as cool as I now am, and would much rather kill them at once, and thus end their sufferings, than have them taken back to slavery and be murdered by piecemeal."

A stunned nation read the headlines in the newspapers on January 28, 1856. The *New York Times* printed a telegram received from Cincinnati: "A stampede of slaves from the border counties of Kentucky took place last night. One slave woman finding escape, cut the throats of her children, and severely wounded others." People grappled with the unimaginable concept of a mercy killing. What would possess a mother to take the life of her own child? Could slavery truly be so evil?

Margaret Garner was arrested in Cincinnati on a criminal charge of murder and her husband and parents for complicity in murder. The Garner trial lasted two weeks. The Garners' lawyers, Jolliffe and Getchell, intended to prevent the Garners from being returned to their master. At first they argued that since the Garners had previously been brought to Ohio by their owner, they were technically free at the time they had tried to escape. The U.S. Commissioner John Pendry who was hearing the case overruled that argument. He found that if the Garners had voluntarily returned to the slave state of Kentucky, they had relinquished their claim to freedom. Jolliffe next wanted the state to have his clients arrested for murder, preventing their return to Kentucky and the clutches of their master, Archibald Gaines. He was fully confident that no court would find the young mother guilty for she had heartily believed it better to free her children's souls than have them endure a life of slavery. A jury would certainly be sympathetic to her plight.

In the end, the rights of the slave owners prevailed over the right of the state of Ohio to seek punishment for murder. Abolitionists appealed to Ohio Governor, Salmon P. Chase, who supported the state of Ohio's claim that the fugitives were free people, but even he could not prevent the Garners' return to slavery. The state's writ of *habeas corpus* compelling the Garners to be brought before the court was ignored by the U.S. marshall. Five weeks after the incident, the Garners were remanded to Archibald Gaines, who then sold them to the Deep South.

As if there had not already been enough tragedy in their family, the ship transporting the Garners had an accident at sea. In the collision some of the slaves who were in chains were hurled overboard. Margaret Garner, with her infant in her arms, either fell into the water or jumped. She was saved, but the baby was drowned. As Margaret saw it, two of her children had now been rescued from a doomed life of slavery.

While some found Margaret Garner's actions to be barbaric, others found them noble. In either case the public was forced to consider the evil effects of slavery. Margaret Garner was never set free until her own death a few years later in 1858 from typhoid fever. She was about twenty-five years old.

Ohio-born author Toni Morrison was inspired by Margaret Garner's horrifying ordeal. Her 1987 Pulitzer Prize–winning novel *Beloved* probably found seeds of inspiration in certain aspects of the young mother's tragic life.

UP A TREE

WITH ONLY SECONDS TO THINK, Charles Gilbert got up on all fours in the dark and began growling and barking like a mad dog. Even he was surprised by the terrifying sounds emanating from his own throat. An intruder had entered the dark confines of the young man's hiding place, and he was literally barking to save his life.

In 1854 Charles Gilbert was living in Richmond, Virginia, one of the largest slave-trading centers on the East Coast. His master, Benjamin Davis, was a notorious slave trader who was always looking to make a profit. It did not break Charles's heart that his cruel master was thinking of selling him; he had suffered enough at his hands. Davis was convinced that he could get a good price for Gilbert. His fine build, his intelligent look, and his "ginger-bread color" were all assets that would help him command a handsome sum. After ads had run for months in the newspapers, however, there had been no takers.

While Davis was busy trying to find a buyer, Charles was trying to find out how to run away. There were rumors of a sympathetic schooner captain from Boston who would take fugitives as passengers. After making the necessary inquiries, Charles learned that if he could make it from Richmond to Old Point Comfort on the Virginia coast he would be smuggled aboard for a fee of ten dollars. Old Point Comfort was on Virginia's east coast where the James River emptied into the Chesapeake Bay.

The distance from where Charles lived in Richmond to Old Point Comfort was roughly eighty miles. He left as soon as the opportunity presented itself, sometime in late July. Davis immediately had slave catchers on his trail. He knew that Charles had lived in Old Point Comfort when he was a young boy and still had family there. He correctly assumed that this was where he was headed. Slave catchers arrived ahead of Charles and began threatening his family. Word quickly spread around town: Anyone assisting Charles would suffer greatly for it.

Davis put up a two-hundred-dollar reward for Charles's capture. Only one brave friend in Old Point Comfort, identified as E. S., defiantly took Charles in for a week, putting his own safety in jeopardy. The slave hunters had intimidated everyone, and Charles had nowhere else to go.

As Charles considered his options, he arrived at the idea of hiding out under the Higee Hotel in Old Point Comfort. The hotel's large frame was not built on a stone foundation but was supported by wooden piers that protruded several feet from the ground at various intervals. They created an expansive crawlspace underneath. The dark, musty place was home to chickens and other animals that scurried about. Left with no other choice Charles Gilbert took refuge in the dank filth under the hotel.

Gilbert made his bed next to the cistern which held the hotel's water supply. For four weeks, in these filthy and cramped living quarters, he survived on the hotel's garbage. He did not dare venture out until the slave hunters had left town. But one evening an unexpected intruder crawled under the hotel with him. Charles lay flat on the ground. In the shadows he could make out the form of a small boy innocently searching for chickens. If the boy came much closer, Charles would be discovered. Immediately Charles crouched on his bent arms and legs and barked ferociously. The terrified youngster clambered out as fast as he could. Charles was satisfied with his quick thinking until he overheard the boy's father say that he would come back and kill the dog.

Charles left that very night, walking over ten miles to Bay Shore near Virginia Beach where he hid in the woods. He concealed himself in the thick underbrush, but at daybreak could see that the cover was insufficient. He climbed up a giant tree and nestled himself securely between the V-shaped branches. For an entire day he racked his brains trying to figure out where to go next.

After a time, he thought of Isabella, a poor washerwoman in Old Point Comfort who might sympathize with the downtrodden. Backtracking, he went directly to her house. She saw his desperate situation and agreed to hide him under the floorboards of her house. Charles's friend John Thomas was the only other one who knew of the arrangement. He stayed in this refuge for two weeks, waiting for the search to die down. Meanwhile he could hear the voices of Isabella and his friend through the floorboards.

At one point six officers arrived, tramping through the house and accusing Isabella of hiding Davis's runaway. One of the men offered John Thomas twenty-five dollars for any information, but both Thomas and Isabella claimed to know nothing about the missing slave's whereabouts.

This close encounter with being recaptured prompted Charles to go back to the Higee Hotel for another stay, thus relieving his friends of the danger they had put themselves in. After one week he left for the isolated forested area located behind the cottage of a man named Stephen Allen. He hoped to find some impenetrable hiding places in the woods. He hid in the dense thicket for just one day before an old man drew close, giving him a start. Fearing discovery, Gilbert once again barked ferociously from his hiding spot in the underbrush, watching with satisfaction as the old man hobbled off.

Charles heard that slave hunters were still actively searching the area around Richmond, Petersburg, and Old Point Comfort—the same areas Charles had been roaming around during the night. So far he had eluded his captors, but the stress was wearing on him. His next refuge was a marsh near the Great Dismal Swamp. This turned out to be a poor choice due to the stench, the mosquitoes, and the snakes that lived there. After just two hours he returned to the Higee Hotel for a third time. After a two-day stay Charles appealed to his mother for help. She finally could no longer stand to see her son in such a dire situation, and no matter the risk she vowed to help him. She had saved a little bit of money, and she gave it now to her son. An overjoyed Charles planned to use the money to board a vessel heading for Philadelphia, Pennsylvania, where he'd heard the Anti-Slavery Society assisted all runaways.

Charles Gilbert had just one more day and night in Virginia before leaving for freedom. He went back to the washhouse to spend his last hours there. He had intended to stay under Isabella's floorboards, but after three hours the coast seemed clear. He went up to an upstairs bedroom. It had been so long since he'd had any semblance of comfort. Then came a pounding on the door of the house. Three officers insisted on searching the premises. While questioning Isabella, who attempted to stall as best she could, one of the officers tramped upstairs, opening the door to Charles's room.

Charles stepped out from behind a thin curtain that served as a room divider and walked right past the officer. He sashayed down the stairs in an old calico dress and bonnet, completely done up in a woman's attire. Isabella did not blink an eye.

The officer inquired, "Whose gal are you?" Charles's entire future, his precious freedom, depended on not just his answer, but on his elevated, evenly pitched, feminine voice. Exuding confidence, Charles nonchalantly replied, "Mr. Cockling's, sir." When asked her name, he replied, "Delie, sir." After what may have seemed like an eternity, the officer offered up the sweetest three words Charles Gilbert had ever heard, "Go on then!" Charles walked right out of the washhouse to begin his new life.

Charles Gilbert paid a thirty-dollar fee and boarded the vessel for Philadelphia. Disappointed to hear that it was not a direct route, he was forced to take cover during a four-week layover in Norfolk, Virginia. By that time the reward Davis had posted in the Richmond newspapers for his capture had increased to $550. When the steamer finally pulled into Philadelphia on November 11, 1854, Davis's men were still searching for him back in Virginia.

Like many travelers on the Underground Railroad, Charles Gilbert's journey to freedom was impossibly difficult. It took more than three-and-a-half months, and required ingenuity, bravery, and endurance before he finally reached his goal.

UNDERGROUND RAILROAD
FACTS AND TRIVIA

It is estimated that from forty thousand to one hundred thousand slaves escaped bondage, with a large portion going through the state of Ohio on their way to Canada.

William Still, a free black man in Pennsylvania, was known as the "Father of the Underground Railroad."

Most Underground Railroad station houses did not have secret rooms and spaces but used existing hiding spaces such as attics, barns, cellars, or closets.

The fall was generally the best time to run north. Crops provided food along the journey and the cornfields provided cover for hiding.

More than four million slaves were set free when the Civil War ended in 1865.

Spirituals such as "When I'm Gone" and "Wade in the Water, Children" were used as codes to inform others about slaves escaping.

Levi Coffin, a white Quaker in Indiana, was known as the "President of the Underground Railroad."

It was common practice for slave families to be part slave, part free, as they purchased their freedom one member at a time.

A slave caught by a patroller without a pass could be whipped. By law slaves were considered runaways if they were apprehended outside a given distance from where they lived. Each state set the distance.

Gangs of kidnappers, especially in the mid-Atlantic states, made money by kidnapping free blacks and selling them into slavery.

Twelve American presidents owned slaves, and eight of them owned slaves while serving as president.

Importing slaves into the United States was a federal crime after 1808, but smuggling continued until the Civil War.

Abolitionist Thomas Garrett worked on the Underground Railroad for forty years and was convicted of harboring fugitive slaves. After receiving a fine of $5,400 in 1848 (which nearly bankrupted him), he brazenly told the judge that he would put a second story on his house so that he could assist more runaways.

Slave families were divided when the master of a plantation died and his estate (including his slave property) was divided up among his heirs. Slaves were used to obtain credit and pay off debts.

Aiding fugitives was a criminal offense, but states varied in their punishment. A conviction could carry a penalty of six months in jail, a thousand dollar fine, and a civil liability of one thousand dollars for each fugitive. Such convictions damaged a person's reputation and social standing in the community.

Slaves who could not tolerate their living conditions sometimes went on strike or were "lying out." They temporarily ran away, and word was sent to their masters that unless a certain condition was met, they would run away permanently.

Philadelphia, Pennsylvania, boasted the nation's first formally organized antislavery society.

Freed slaves had to carry their free papers with them at all times in case they were questioned. The papers needed to be updated for a fee, which increased the coffers of the state.

According to Wilbur H. Siebert, a foremost authority, there were more than 3,200 documented people who worked on the Underground Railroad.

Canada became a safe haven for escaping slaves after the passage of antislavery legislation on July 9, 1793. After the War of 1812, the news circulated that Canada was a safe haven for slaves on the run.

The American Anti-Slavery Society, with both black and white members, was formed in 1833 to heighten awareness of the injustices of slavery and to support its abolition. Within five years it had a quarter of a million members.

By law the children followed the status of their mother. If she was free when they were born, they were free as well; if she was a slave, they too were born slaves.

In 1777 Vermont became the first state to abolish slavery.

Calvin Fairbank was arrested twice for taking fugitive slaves over the Ohio River to freedom. He was given a fifteen-year sentence, the longest given to an Underground Railroad activist.

In 1859, 16 percent of the total United States population was black.

The most heavily traveled route along the Underground Railroad went through Ohio, Indiana, and western Pennsylvania.

Slavery was abolished in the British Empire, including Canada, in 1833.

The American Colonization Society, founded in 1816, established the colony of Liberia, where freed slaves were removed to settle their own community on the west coast of Africa.

Warring African tribes attacked their enemies and sold or traded their prisoners of war to European slave dealers. In 1619 the Dutch sold slaves to settlers in Jamestown, the first permanent English settlement in North America.

Slavery existed in America from the earliest period of colonial settlement at the beginning of the seventeenth century until it was abolished in 1865 by passage of the Thirteenth Amendment.

Ohio was a center of high activity on the Underground Railroad because it bordered the slave states of Kentucky and Virginia, and it was linked to Canada by Lake Erie.

After the passage of the Fugitive Slave Act of 1850, many blacks fled to Canada. Not all of them returned to the United States after slavery was abolished in 1865.

Serious scholars refute the claim that patterned quilts had encoded messages that showed the way to freedom.

The National Underground Railroad Network to Freedom, Omaha, Nebraska, in association with National Parks Service (NPS), lists sites that have approved documentation in connection with the Underground Railroad. There are currently 181 sites, 45 programs, and 34 facilities in 26 states and the District of Columbia.

BIBLIOGRAPHY

Books

Abajian, James de T., comp. *Blacks in Selected Newspapers, Censuses and Other Sources: An Index to Names and Subjects.* Vols. 1, 2, 3. Boston: G. K. Hall & Company, 1977.

Andrews, William L., ed. *Narrative of the Life of Frederick Douglass, an American Slave, Written by Himself.* New York: W. W. Norton & Company, 1997.

———. Introduction to *Six Women's Slave Narratives.* New York: Oxford University Press, 1988.

Baker, Roger. *Clara: An Ex-Slave in Gold Rush Colorado.* Central City, Colo.: Black Hawk Publishing, 2003.

Berlin, Ira. *Generations of Captivity: A History of African-American Slaves.* Cambridge, Mass.: The Belknap Press of Harvard University Press, 2003.

Berlin, Ira, Marc Favreau, and Steven F. Miller, eds. *Remembering Slavery: African Americans Talk about Their Personal Experiences of Slavery and Freedom.* New York: The New Press, 1998.

Blassingame, John, ed. *Slave Testimonies: Two Centuries of Letters, Speeches, Interviews, and Autobiographies.* Baton Rouge: Louisiana State University Press, 1977.

Blight, David W., ed. *Passages to Freedom: The Underground Railroad in History and Memory.* Washington, D.C.: Smithsonian Books, 2004.

Blockson, Charles L. *Hippocrene Guide to the Underground Railroad.* New York: Hippocrene Books, 1994.

————. *The Underground Railroad: Dramatic Firsthand Accounts of Daring Escapes to Freedom.* New York: Berkeley Books, 1987.

Bolden, Tonya. *The Book of African-American Women: 150 Crusaders, Creators, and Uplifters.* Holbrook, Mass.: Adams Media, 1996.

Bontemps, Arna. introduction to *Five Black Lives: The Autobiographies of Venture Smith, James Mars, William Grimes, the Reverend G. W. Offley, and James L. Smith.* 1855. Reprint, Middleton, Conn.: Wesleyan University Press, 1971.

————. *Great Slave Narratives.* Boston: Beacon Press, 1969.

Bordewich, Fergus M. *Bound for Canaan: The Underground Railroad and the War for the Soul of America.* New York: Amistad, 2005.

Botkin, Benjamin Albert. *Lay My Burden Down: A Folk History of Slavery.* Chicago: University of Chicago Press, 1945.

Brown, John. *Slave Life in Georgia: A Narrative of the Life, Sufferings, and Escape of John Brown, a Fugitive Slave.* Savannah: The Beehive Press, 1855.

Carbone, Elisa Lynn. *Stealing Freedom.* New York: Random House, 1999.

Century, Douglas. *Toni Morrison.* New York: Chelsea House Publishers, 1994.

Chase, Henry. *In Their Footsteps: The American Visions Guide to African-American Heritage Sites.* New York: Henry Holt, 1948.

Coffin, Levi. *Reminiscences of Levi Coffin, the Reputed President of the Underground Railroad; Being a Brief History of the Labors of a Lifetime in Behalf of the Slave, with the Stories of Numerous Fugitives, Who Gained Their Freedom through His Instrumentality, and Many Other Incidents.* Cincinnati: Western Tract Society, 1876.

Cohen, Anthony. *The Underground Railroad in Montgomery County, Maryland: A History and Driving Guide.* Rockville, Md.: Montgomery County Historical Society, 1995.

Craft, William, and Ellen Craft. *Running a Thousand Miles for Freedom: The Escape of William and Ellen Craft from Slavery.* Athens, Ga.: The University of Georgia Press, 1999. First published 1860 by Brown Thrasher Books, London.

Danforth, Mildred E. *A Quaker Pioneer: Laura Haviland, Superintendent of the Underground.* New York: Exposition Press, 1961.

DeRamus, Betty. *Forbidden Fruit: Love Stories from the Underground Railroad.* New York: Atria Books, 2005.

Douglass, Frederick. *Narrative of the Life of Frederick Douglass, an American Slave, Written by Himself.* New York: New American Library, 1968. First published 1845 by Boston Antislavery Society.

Drayton, Daniel. *Personal Memoir of Daniel Drayton, for Four Years and Four Months a Prisoner (for Charity's Sake) in Washington Jail, Including a Narrative of the Voyage and the Capture of the Schooner Pearl.* 1855. Reprint, New York: Negro Universities Press, 1969.

Dykstra, Robert R. *Bright Radical Star: Black Freedom and White Supremacy on the Hawkeye Frontier.* Ames, Iowa: Iowa State University Press, 1997.

Ex-Slave Narratives. Brooksville, Ky.: Bracken County Historical Society, 2001.

Foner, Philip S. *History of Black Americans from the Compromise of 1850 to the End of the Civil War.* Westport, Conn.: Greenwood Press, 1983.

————. *History of Black Americans from the Emergence of the Cotton Kingdom to the Eve of the Compromise of 1850.* Westport, Conn.: Greenwood Press, 1983.

Fradin, Dennis Brindell. *Bound for the North Star: True Stories of Fugitive Slaves.* New York: Clarion Books, 2000.

Franklin, John Hope, and Alfred A. Moss, Jr. *From Slavery to Freedom.* New York: McGraw-Hill, 2000.

Franklin, John Hope, and Loren Schweninger. *Runaway Slaves: Rebels on the Plantation.* New York: Oxford University Press, 2000.

Gaines, Edith M. *Freedom Light: Underground Railroad Stories from Ripley, Ohio.* Cleveland: New Day Press, 1991.

Gates, Henry Louis, Jr., foreword to *Unchained Memories: Readings from* The Slave Narratives. Boston: Bulfinch Press, 2002.

Goodall, Hurley C., compiler. *Underground Railroad: The Invisible Road to Freedom through Indiana.* Indiana: Works Progress Administration Writers Project, 2000.

Grover, Kathryn. *The Fugitive's Gibraltar: Escaping Slaves and Abolitionism in New Bedford, Massachusetts.* Amherst: University of Massachusetts Press, 2001.

Hagedorn, Ann. *Beyond the River: The Untold Story of the Heroes of the Underground Railroad.* New York: Simon & Schuster, 2002.

Hamilton, Virginia. *The People Could Fly: American Black Folktales.* New York: Knopf, 1985.

Harris, Middleton, compiler, with the assistance of Morris Levitt, Roger Furman, [and] Ernest Smith. *The Black Book.* New York: Random House, Inc., 1974.

Haviland, Laura S. *A Woman's Work: Labors and Experiences of Laura S. Haviland 1808-1898.* Cincinnati: Walden & Stowe, 1882.

Helper, Hinton Rowan. *The Impending Crisis of the South.* New York: A. B. Burdick, 1857.

Hendrick, George and Willene. *Fleeing for Freedom: Stories of the Underground Railroad.* Chicago: Ivan R. Dee, 2004.

Hilty, Hiram H. *By Land and by Sea: Quakers Confront Slavery and Its Aftermath in North Carolina.* Greensboro: North Carolina Friends Historical Society, 1993.

Hoobler, Dorothy, and Thomas Hoobler. *The African American Family Album.* New York: Oxford City Press, 1995.

Horton, James Oliver, and Lois E. Horton. *Slavery and the Making of America.* Oxford: Oxford University Press, 2005.

Hurmence, Belinda, ed. *Forty-Eight Oral Histories of Former North and South Carolina Slaves.* New York: Penguin Books, 1990.

Jones, Friday. *Days of Bondage: Autobiography of Friday Jones, Being a Brief Narrative of His Trials and Tribulations in Slavery.* Washington, D.C.: Commercial Publishing Co., 1883.

Kallen, Stuart A. *The Way People Live: Life on the Underground Railroad.* San Diego: Lucent Books, 2000.

Landau, Elaine. *Slave Narratives: The Journey to Freedom.* New York: Franklin Watts, 2001.

Lowery, Linda. *One More Valley, One More Hill: The Story of Aunt Clara Brown.* New York: Random House, 2002.

Lucas, Marion Brunson. *A History of Blacks in Kentucky from Slavery to Segregation, 1760–1891.* Frankfort: Kentucky Historical Society, 2003.

Maruyama, Susan J. *Perseverance: African Americans, Voices of Triumph.* Alexandria, Va.: Time-Life Books, 1993.

McDougall, Marion Gleason. *Fugitive Slaves 1619-1865.* New York: Bergman Publishers, 1969.

Mellon, James, ed. *Bullwhip Days: The Slaves Remember: An Oral History.* New York: Avon Books, 1990.

Miller, Randall M. *"Dear Master": Letters of a Slave Family.* Ithaca, N.Y.: Cornell University Press, 1978.

Miller, Ruth. *Black American Literature, 1760–Present.* New York: Macmillan, 1971.

Nichols, Charles H. *Black Men in Chains.* New York: Lawrence Hill & Co., 1972.

———. *Many Thousand Gone: The Ex-Slaves' Account of Their Bondage and Freedom.* Leiden, Germany: E. J. Brill, 1963.

Nine, Darlene Clark. *Black Women in American History from Colonial Times through the Nineteenth Century.* Brooklyn, N.Y.: Carlson Publishing, 1990.

Paynter, John H. *Fugitives of Daniel Drayton.* New York: AMS Press, 1930.

Perdue, Charles L., Jr., Thomas E. Barden, and Robert K. Phillips, eds. *Weevils in the Wheat.* Charlottesville: University Press of Virginia, 1976.

Pickard, Kate. *The Kidnapped and the Ransomed.* New York: Negro University Press, 1968.

Rappaport, Doreen. *Freedom River.* New York: Jump at the Sun Hyperion Books for Children, 2000.

Rankin, Reverend John. *Letters on American Slavery Addressed to Mr. Thomas Rankin, Merchant at Middlebrook, Augusta County, Virginia.* Boston: Garrison & Knapp, 1833; and Isaac Knapp, 5th ed., 1839.

Rawick, George, P., ed. *The American Slave: A Composite Autobiography.* Federal Writers' Project. Westport, Conn.: Greenwood Publishing Co., 1972.

Schlissel, Lillian. *Black Frontiers: A History of African-American Heroes in the Old West.* New York, New York: Simon & Schuster Books for Young Readers, 1995.

Schneider, Dorothy, and Carl J. Schneider. *An Eyewitness History of Slavery in America from Colonial Times to the Civil War.* New York: Checkmark Books, 2000.

Seibert, Wilbur Henry. *The Underground Railroad from Slavery to Freedom.* New York: Russell & Russell, 1967.

Silag, Bill, ed. *Outside In: African-American History in Iowa 1838–2000.* Des Moines, State Historical Society of Iowa, 2001.

Smedley, Robert C. *History of the Underground Railroad in Chester and the Neighboring Counties of Pennsylvania.* 1883. Reprint, New York: Negro Universities Press, 1968.

Smith, James L. *Autobiography of James L. Smith, Including, Also, Reminiscences of Slave Life, Recollections of the War, Education of Freedmen, Causes of the Exodus, Etc.* Miami: Mnemosyne

Publishing Co., Inc, 1969. First published 1881 by Press of the Bulletin Company, Norwich, Connecticut.

———. *Recollections of a Former Slave.* New York: Humanity Books, 2004.

Smith, Jessie Carney, ed. *Epic Lives: One Hundred Black Women Who Made a Difference.* Detroit: Visible Ink Press, 1993.

Sprague, Stuart Seely, ed. *The Autobiography of John P. Parker, His Promised Land.* New York: W.W. Norton & Company, 1996.

Steele, James. *Freedom's River: The African-American Contribution to Democracy.* Chicago: Franklin Watts, 1994.

Sterling, Dorothy, ed. *We Are Your Sisters: Black Women in the Nineteenth Century.* New York: W. W. Norton & Company, 1984.

Still, William. *The Underground Railroad.* Chicago: Johnson Publishing Company, Inc., 1970.

Stowe, Harriet Beecher. *A Key to Uncle Tom's Cabin: Presenting the Original Facts and Documents upon Which the Story Is Founded. Together with Corroborative Statements Verifying the Truth of the Work.* Boston: John P. Jewett & Co., 1853.

Strother, Horatio T. *The Underground Railroad in Connecticut.* Middleton, Conn.: Wesleyan University Press, 1962.

Stroyer, Jacob. *My Life in the South in Five Slave Narratives, a Compendium.* New York: Arno Press and The New York Times, 1968.

Switala, William J. *Underground Railroad in Delaware, Maryland, and West Virginia.* Mechanicsburg, Pa.: Stackpole Books, 2004.

Talmadge, Marian. *Barney Ford, Black Baron.* New York: Dodd, Mead & Company, 1973.

Thompson, Dr. L.S. *The Story of Mattie J. Jackson: Her Parentage, Experience of Eighteen Years in Slavery, Incidents during the War, Her Escape from Slavery: A True Story.* Lawrence, Mass.: Printed at Sentinel Office, 1866.

Troester, Rosalie Riegle, ed. *Historic Women of Michigan: A Sesquicentennial Celebration.* Lansing, Mich.: Michigan Women's Studies Association, 1987.

Yetman, Norman, R. *Life Under the "Peculiar Institution"; Selections from the Slave Narrative Collection.* New York: Holt, Rinehart and Winston, 1970.

Brochures

Exploring a Common Past: Researching and Interpreting the Underground Railroad, by the U.S. Department of the Interior, National Park Service, History Office, National Register, History, and Education, 1998.

Historic Ripley, Ohio Freedom's Landing Underground Railroad Tour. Brown County, Department of Economic Development, Ohio, 2004.

John P. Parker 1827–1900. The John P. Parker Historical Society.

Mary "Polly" Johnson 1784–1871. New Bedford, Mass.: New Bedford Historical Society.

Rankin House: Home of Reverend John Rankin Abolitionist Freedom's Hero. Ripley, Ohio: Ripley Heritage, Inc., 1970.

The Underground Railroad: New Bedford, Mass.: New Bedford Whaling National Historical Park.

Magazines

Beal, M. Gertrude. "The Underground Railroad in Guilford County," *The Southern Friend* 2, no. 1 (Spring 1980): 18–28.

Berrier, G. Galin. "The Slaves of Ruel Daggs." The Iowa Griot publication of the African American Historical Museum and Cultural Center of Iowa, Cedar Rapids, Iowa, (Summer 2002): 6–7.

Blockson, Charles L. "Escape from Slavery: The Underground Railroad. *National Geographic* (July 1984): 2–39.

Chase, Henry. "Plotting a Course for Freedom; Paul Jennings: White House Memoirist-Servant of President James Madison; Special Issue: The Untold Story of Blacks in the White House." *American Visions* 10, no. 1 (February–March 1995):52–54.

Coon, Diane Perrine. "Great Escapes: The Underground Railroad." *Northern Kentucky Heritage* 9, no. 2 (Spring/Summer 2002): 2–12.

Garretson, Owen A. "The Underground Railroad in Iowa." *Iowa Journal of History and Politic* (July 1924): 91.

Hatcher, Susan Tucker. "North Carolina Quakers: Bona Fide Abolitionists." *The Southern Friend* 1, no. 2 (Autumn 1979): 81–96.

Paynter, John H. "The Fugitives of the Pearl." *Journal of Negro History* I (July 1916): 243–64.

"The Underground Railroad Freedom Center." *Ebony* (November 2004): 46–49.

Williams-Meyers, A. J. "Some Notes on the Extent of New York City's Involvement in the Underground Railroad." *Afro-Americans in New York Life and History* (July 2005): 73.

Newspapers

Chrastina, Paul, "Disguised As a White Man, Slave Takes Her Husband North." *Old News* (Landisville, Penn.) 1860.

Libby, Sam. "Jail Hill's Rich History Is Reborn in Research." *New York Times,* March 28, 1999.

Ricks, Mary Kay. "Escape on the Pearl." *The Washington Post,* August 12, 1998.

"Slave-Hunters in Boston." *Old Liberator,* November 1, 1850.

"Some Boy to Attend Tech." *The New Bedford Sunday Standard,* December 15, 1918.

Other

African-American Records of Bracken County, Kentucky: 1797-1999. Brooksville, Ky.: Bracken County Historical Society, Vol. 1, 2000. Caroline Miller.

American History Series: A Slave's Story: Running a Thousand Miles to Freedom. VHS. Learning Corporation of America. Columbus, Ohio, 1990.

Broadway Christian Church deed. Germantown, Kentucky, 1880.

Found Voices: The Slave Narratives. VHS. Films for the Humanities and Sciences, Princeton, N.J., 1999.

Slave Voices—Things Past Telling. VHS. Smart-Grosvenor, Vertamae. Produced and distributed by DIVE AUDIO, Beverly Hills, Calif., 1992.

Web sites

"The African American Mosaic: A Library of Congress Resource Guide for the Study of Black History & Culture." lcweb.loc .gov/exhibits/african/intro.html.

"Born in Slavery: Slave Narratives from the Federal Writers' Project, 1936–1938." A joint presentation of the Manuscript and Prints and Photographs Divisions of the Library of Congress. memory.loc.gov/ammem/snhtml/snhome.html.

Carpenter, Marian. "Sailin' to Freedom: Water Routes and Vessels on the Underground Railroad in Maryland." www.freedomcenter.org.

"Documenting the American South." Chapel Hill, North Carolina: Academic Affairs Library, University of North Carolina at Chapel Hill. docsouth.unc.edu/.

Duke University Library Web site. Durham, North Carolina. library.duke.edu.

Kozel, Scott M. "Chesapeake and Delaware Canal." Pennways, Roads to the Future. Accessed July 5, 2004. www.pennways .com/CD_Canal.html.

"National Underground Railroad Network to Freedom." National Park Service. 209.10.16.21/template/frontend/index.cfm.

"Pathways to Freedom: Maryland & the Underground Railroad." Maryland Public Television, 2002. pathways.thinkport.org/ flash_home.cfm

"Lest We Forget: The Triumph over Slavery." Archives and Special Collections. Schomburg Center for Research in Black Culture. The New York Public Library, 2004. digital.nypl.org/lwf/ flash.html.

INDEX

ABOUT THE AUTHOR

Tricia Martineau Wagner, a North Carolina author and presenter, is an experienced elementary teacher and reading specialist. The Ohio native is a well-versed and entertaining speaker who brings history to life. Ms. Wagner enjoys conducting classrooms presentations on the subject matter in her books as well as creative writing for grades two through twelve.

This is Tricia's third book for TwoDot, an imprint of the Globe Pequot Press. Her two other titles are *It Happened on the Oregon Trail* and *African-American Women of the Old West*. Tricia makes her home in Charlotte, North Carolina, with her husband, Mark, their children, Kelsey and Mitch, and their puppy, Tiger.

She can be reached at trishmwagner@earthlink.net.